The Intercultural Exeter Couples Model

The Intercultural Exeter Couples Model

Making Connections for a Divided World Through Systemic-Behavioral Therapy

Janet Reibstein
Reenee Singh

Registered Offices
John Wiley & Sons, Inc., 111 River Street, Hoboken, NJ 07030, USA
John Wiley & Sons Ltd, The Atrium, Southern Gate, Chichester, West Sussex, PO19 8SQ, UK

Editorial Office
111 River Street, Hoboken, NJ 07030, USA

For details of our global editorial offices, customer services, and more information about Wiley products visit us at www.wiley.com.

Wiley also publishes its books in a variety of electronic formats and by print-on-demand. Some content that appears in standard print versions of this book may not be available in other formats.

Library of Congress Cataloging-in-Publication data is available
9781119668411 (Paperback); 9781119668428 (ePDF); 9781119668435 (epub)

Cover Design: Wiley
Cover Image: © Bruce Rolff/Shutterstock

Set in 10/12pt JansonText by SPi Global, Pondicherry, India

SKY47B32AAF-36F5-4342-B245-AD988EF341BE_110920

Contents

PART 1

The Model and Its Development

CHAPTER 1

Introduction

The public debut of the Intercultural Exeter Model (IEM) at the annual conference of the UK's Association for Family Therapy in 2017 was in the year that Prince Harry and Meghan Markle announced their engagement, and, with that, came a worldwide, populist interest, an interest not ever before so publicly recorded in the area of intercultural couples. This striking public attention put the focus on something we, the authors, along with others working in this field for years already knew: there is a dearth of either research on, or reports of, best clinical practice about working with couples of this sort. How do you do it and do it well?

Indeed, most clinical models of couples work do not even nod to the contribution culture will make to any of the myriad presenting conditions people need help with. Those clinicians working systemically will know that an exception has been within systemic theorizing (e.g., Falicov, 2014; Gabb & Singh, 2015b). Broadly, systemic theory explicitly encourages practitioners to be aware of culture, both pointed to in a general way and a more specified one by referring to the ways in which gender, race, religion, age, sexuality, ethnicity, and class shape experience (Burnham, 2012); and more particularly as a background to specific events in the Coordinated Management of Meaning (CMM) model that also denotes ways in which culture, events, and cultural beliefs contribute to people's reality (Pearce, 2007). However, despite this admirable emphasis on cultural context and consequence, therapists need more. There has been no systematic effort to translate systemic ideas that take into account a cultural perspective into working with couples. None has existed to enable the clinician both to focus on and utilize data about cultural differences in a theorized way, or even in a way that incorporates other existing clinical tools to adapt them specifically to address cultural differences.

The Intercultural Exeter Couples Model: Making Connections for a Divided World Through Systemic-Behavioral Therapy, First Edition. Janet Reibstein and Reenee Singh.
© 2021 John Wiley & Sons Ltd. Published 2021 by John Wiley & Sons Ltd.

This is a significant and gaping hole in working with couples who come from different cultures. That is the raison d'être for this book: it describes a method that helps clinicians to do so.

There is another purpose to the book: to join up best practice, to make the systemic behavioral and the behavioral systemic. There has been work with couples in which both behavioral/cognitive behavioral therapy (CBT) approaches and systemic ones have had much to contribute to ameliorate distress in a variety of conditions (cf. Reibstein & Burbach, 2012, 2013). But till now there have not been attempts to marry up these two approaches. The systemic one has the potential impact of being in a couple on capacity to make changes when there is psychological distress in at least one member of the couple (cf. Reibstein & Burbach, 2013). Because of this it has much of value to contribute. Meanwhile, hardy research has shown the value of using particular behavioral interventions, both purely behavioral and CBT, in reducing distress (cf. Reibstein & Burbach, 2012, 2013).

Indeed, specifically in the treatment of depression the value of both approaches was enshrined by the UK's NICE (National Institute for Clinical Excellence) Guidelines in 2009. In Chapter 2 we detail how significant the UK government's approach, through its NICE, has been. It has been so in helping to validate, standardize, and make accountable clinical work, in general. But we point out also how this approach has both contributed to but also handicapped the development of innovative and effective new models of therapy. Despite the NICE 2009 validation given to the systemic approach to couples therapy, specifically around depression, and to particular interventions that stem from a behavioral approach, this NICE approach left a question: How do you join them in a comprehensive way? The original Exeter Model (EM), which we describe below (Reibstein & Sherbersky, 2012), was in fact developed to do this.

The impact of cultural differences began to emerge as the EM evolved both within its original clinic. But this was increasingly more pertinently visible outside, in settings across the UK where diversity and its impact began to emerge among the clients presenting at practitioners' offices. And as it did, it became clear that the question of the impact of culture—something we intuitively know to be the case—still remained unaddressed. In consequence we began adapting the EM to begin to fill that hole, yielding the IEM.

The IEM now addresses, front and center, using best couple practice techniques, how to work explicitly with the differing cultural aspects of people's lives. In our global world, in a world of multicultural families and couples, in which children of couples who partner across cultures increasingly are raised within a hybridity of cultures, this is imperative. To avoid doing this is tantamount to avoiding something as basic as age, gender, abilities, sexualities, or income, language or educational constraints or privileges: in other words, the very seeds of people's actual, lived, daily lives. For couples, most essentially, the meshing or clashing of the cultural can be the often unexamined heart of misunderstandings instead of becoming the source of great enrichment.

Our current rhetoric of love does not really allow the consciousness of difference to become part of our discourse around intimate relationships. These result in a denial of the actuality of romantic life: conflict is an inevitable fact of couples' reality. As John Gottman's research has so clearly shown (cf. Gottman, 1994), all couples need to learn how to manage conflict between themselves. Leaving out how to think about and work with the cultural difference within a couple in a couple training, therefore, is at the very least ignorant. At its worst, it's irresponsible. Hence the IEM, the evolution of the EM.

There are two urgent, major, and progressive themes calling ever more loudly and persistently through current developments in therapy theory, practice, and training—particularly within work with families and couples. Firstly, there is the need to work sensitively, wisely, and constructively and be attentive to differences in cultures within relationships that present in the therapy room. Secondly, there is the need to become able to work within evidence-based practices that can cut across different schools of psychotherapy. That is, to be aware, or part of, a "third wave" of psychotherapy practice that unites themes and practices across formerly divided trainings. A currently well-equipped clinician should be able to employ and understand techniques and ideas from a range of therapies, using these in a way that is coherent with their basic therapeutic training and stance. A currently well-equipped clinician should be able to understand and be alert to nuances of cultural differences that will necessarily be playing out within couples and families that present for therapy, or that an individual brings in their individual narrative as it may unfold within the therapy room for individual therapy. Yet there has been no single coherent model of therapy theory, training, and practice, until now, that unites these two major themes. There is still no training that can thus prepare a therapist to practice in this way.

THE ORIGINAL EM

The original EM arose in response to the NICE recommendation in 2009 for using *behavioral* couple treatment for depression. We italicize "behavioral" as that points specifically to the contribution of behavioral methods to the recommendation, while the statement itself, implies the importance of a systemic approach:

> A time-limited, psychological intervention derived from a model of the interactional processes in relationships where the intervention aims to help participants understand the effects of their interactions on each other as

factors in the development and/or maintenance of symptoms and problems. The aim is to change the nature of the interactions so that they may develop more supportive and less conflictual relationships.

(National Institute of Clinical Excellence [NICE], 2009)

This statement is a systemic one: it underscores that the couple dynamic is an important part of the change mechanism, in this case for depression. Other research has found this to be so for other conditions (cf. Baucom, Whisman, & Paprocki, 2012). This is thought to be due, in part, to the effects of continuous, daily reinforcement of habit change within the intimate, real life of an ongoing domestic relationship. The evidence being amassed by CBT researchers on couples work in depression specifically has put couples therapy on that treatment map (Snyder & Halford, 2012). But systemic workers and thinkers have useful ideas and techniques to offer.

That this is so was pointed to in an early article by Hafner and his co-authors that partners can aid therapy (Hafner, Badenoch, Fisher, & Swift, 1983) as well as in research discussed by Snyder and Halford (2012) who provide a comprehensive overview of research on the effectiveness of couples therapy not only for relationship distress, but also for a variety of individual physical and mental health problems. On the flip side, problems are also maintained through reinforcement of habits within couple and family relationships, and there is also established evidence that relationship distress is associated with the onset or maintenance, or both, of mental health problems (Parker, Johnson, & Ketring, 2012).

The EM was developed in an attempt to make systemic work more empirically sound: it resonates with past work that has been empirically verified. That is, its interventions are all ones that have been either validated as "gold standard" ones from (behavioral therapy) randomly controlled research trials (RCTs) or from the validation by a group of experts in current couples therapy practice. Therefore, the non-behavioral, empathy-based interventions it uses are ones validated by a convened Expert Reference Group to establish best practice for NHS commissioned work and for externally validated training courses (Pilling, Roth, & Stratton, 2010; Stratton, Reibstein, Lask, Singh, & Asen, 2011). The EM became a systemic-behavioral training and practice and was developed by Janet Reibstein and Hannah Sherbersky at the University of Exeter. It was created within the School of Psychology, Clinical Education Development And Research (CEDAR) programme and its Accessing Evidence-Based Psychological Therapies (AccEPT) clinical training clinic. It was subsequently rolled out and has been in practice since 2010 in numerous settings, both within that university clinic, various NHS services across the UK, and within private practices.

A manual was drawn up by Reibstein and Sherbersky (2010) for use for both research projects and for training within a pilot training clinic for both MSc in Systemic Practice and Doctorate in Clinical Psychology students within the University of Exeter. This clinic ran for 4 years, treating couples in which at least one member of the couple had a diagnosis of depression. They were referred to the clinic either through their NHS GP practices or the local depression treatment services. As a manualized model it could more easily go on to be able to be validated, as a whole therapy approach, in itself. The EM also was part of a general trend in third wave CBT which emphasizes the salience of empathy (e.g., Gilbert, 2010; Hayes, Luoma, Bond, Masuda, & Lillis, 2006; Linehan, 1993; Lynch, Trost, Salsman, & Linehan, 2007); these approaches fuse various behavioral techniques with those that develop empathy. The emphasis on both of these things—empathy and behavior—were reflected in the interventions, which were roughly categorized as "systemic-behavioral" or "systemic-empathic." Indeed, the EM, while explicitly utilizing behavioral interventions, was also in other ways resonant with other systemic couples therapy models, one prominent one being Emotionally Focused Couples Therapy (Johnson et al., 2005), which, of course, emphasizes the need to strengthen the empathic connection within the couple. Interestingly, a number of years before the publication of the work coming from Johnson's lab around this the research team of Jacobson and Christensen, coming from a behavioral tradition, had also emphasized the need for therapists to work on this area. Their research showed that, without such an emphasis, any initial progress made would deteriorate over time (Jacobson & Christenson, 1998).

The NICE statement was based on the "best available" evidence, which equates to "gold standard" researched treatments: that is, RCTs. Only a handful of these past research endeavors approached the "gold standard." These were all on behavioral couples therapy, yielding specifically behavioral interventions that formed the specifically approved interventions. However, there is, of course, a problem using only these to reflect best practice on the ground. That is largely because of the difficulty of funding, the problem of establishing quantifiable variables, and the length of time incurred in carrying out and publishing RCT research. This issue is enlarged upon in Chapter 2. In consequence, a less-than gold standard methodology to establish "best current practice" was carried out within a government-sponsored effort through the use of an Expert Reference Group. In this, nominated seasoned and research-savvy practitioners in couples therapy agreed on current best practice interventions (see University College London (UCL) Core Competences, Couple Therapy for Depression webpage[1]).

Because there has been more research on the effectiveness of couples therapy for depression than for other mental or physical health conditions there have been a number of different couples therapy modalities for treating

---

[1] JR was advisor to this group to ensure a systemic perspective was included.

depression. These have included the original purely behavioral, Behavioral Couples Therapy (cf. Gottman, Notarius, Gonso, & Markman, 1976; Jacobson & Margolin, 1979). Such models taught direct, clear communication skills; conflict management skills; utilized behavioral exchange and problem-solving skills; and were programmatic and time-limited.

While these behavioral interventions demonstrated effectiveness, Integrative Behavioral Couples Therapy (Jacobson & Christenson, 1998) was developed to address the fact that effectiveness tended to fade after about a year. This newer model added in "Acceptance/Tolerance" work. Indeed, adding in interventions that increased "acceptance" and "tolerance" (i.e., gaining understanding, apprehending respective limitations) yielded longer lasting effects. Acceptance and tolerance work was about increasing the ability to understand each other, empathically, and to being able, through this, to make adaptations to each other. This meant embracing the other's limits and limitations, yielding a more generous tolerance as well as better emotional understanding. In the EM the interventions that increased such understanding—that is, the ones nominated by the Expert Reference Group that did so—were added to those validated in the behavioral couples work. So the EM encompasses specific behavioral and specific empathic interventions, as will be delineated below.

Other couples therapy modalities have included a previous attempt to integrate behavioral and systemic, using a less comprehensive and at that point not as clearly validated set of behavioral techniques and systemic ones: that is, Behavioral-Systemic Couples Therapy (Crowe & Ridley, 1990), and also Systemic Couples Therapy (e.g., Jones & Asen, 2000), which did not specify specific interventions.

The EM took as its starting point the systemic proposition underlying the NICE guidelines statement. It then created a rubric of best practice interventions that could be subsumed within that systemic proposition. These could be divided into "systemic behavioral" (which were from the "gold standard" research papers and endorsed within the Expert Reference Group (ERG) description) and "systemic empathic" (which were from the ERG description). The EM idea was to make systemic behavioral and behavioral systemic. It extends behavioral techniques that have been shown to be effective treating depression, but—crucially—framing them within a systemic lens.

The original EM, after formulating this fusion of behavioral and systemic ideas into its investigation of the circularities of behaviors, thoughts, and feelings that become reinforced within a couple, leading to the often unwitting reinforcement of depression, uses the following interventions, each of which were either cited as "gold standard" ones for depression (and so are "behavioral") by NICE, or as agreed upon "best practice" ones by the ERG (and, in the main, are "empathic" interventions):

Systemic Empathic	Systemic Behavioral
Reframing	Circularities
Genograms	Enactments
Interviewing internalized other	
Circular questioning	Communication training
Translating meaning	Problem solving
Creating safe space for exploration	
Empathic bridging maneuvers	Homework tasks
Investigating family scripts	Behavioral exchange
Investigating attachment narratives	Communication skills training

The model combines both these approaches (behavioral and systemic). But it sets as its rationale that stated in the NICE statement: the maintenance cycle of the couple system is the fulcrum of treatment. Change comes about through effective disruption of the maintenance cycle. This disruption comes about through the skillful deployment of the validated interventions, but within a context that sees things systemically.

The key invention of the EM however is its concatenation of the idea of a *couple's maintenance cycle*—that is, that they reinforce each other through their responses to each other—with the CBT one of the *thoughts–feelings–behavior feedback loop maintenance cycle*. This is a fusion of CBT and systemic. It will be enlarged upon in Chapter 3 and illustrated in Part 2 of the book. It teaches the therapists how to describe a *couple's maintenance cycle*. It asks each member of the couple about the behaviors they are reacting to in relation to each other, but asks them also to reveal—and subsequently, together interrogate—the reactive sequence of hidden, unspoken thoughts and feelings that accompany the seen or spoken behaviors. The unspoken parts of the maintenance cycle become the vehicles for revelations to the other member of the couple, who characteristically might have been making inaccurate assumptions and attributions about the observable behaviors and reacting to them inaccurately. Investigating why and how they have the reactions, through the use of the (validated) interventions within the EM, in their thoughts and feelings, becomes revelatory for the couple and, in narrative terms, frees them to create a different story, as other possible ones can emerge.

The couple's maintenance cycle has as its focus how the interactive cycle of responses to each other maintains whatever the presenting problem may be. (In the case of its use in the training clinic, this was depression). Its assumption is that this cycle maintains the problem, most often unwittingly. Indeed, often couples who come in for treatment of a problem have a caring, loving relationship, yet are *unwittingly* doing behaviors and/or making distorting assumptions about what the other wants, needs, thinks, and feels out of benign motives that in fact *maintain* the presenting problem. Examining the maintenance cycle asks what it is—perhaps unwittingly—in a couple's interactions that are maintaining the symptom. In this the model is purely systemic and differs from many other forms of the use of couples therapy, in which couple distress is assumed or meant to be the presenting feature to qualify for couple intervention. In the EM and IEM the couple may be very supportive of each other, unwittingly maintaining unhelpful things. Unlike many other forms of couples therapy, to use the model, therefore, couple dysfunction is not a prerequisite; in fact, just being *in* a couple is the only one.

Couples were seen in the University of Exeter clinic mainly for from 6 to 18 sessions for treatment of depression. Trainees in the EM from outside the university brought it into use to treat other issues. These were those that present within the NHS IAPT (Integrated Access to Psychological Therapy) services; private therapy treatment for couple dissatisfaction, sexual problems, and other couple issues; within a pilot treatment program for alcohol and substance abuse; in NHS CAMHS—Children and Adolescent Mental Health Services—(for the treatment of couple dysfunction within family therapy settings); and in outpatient services such as crisis intervention services and older adult services.

But, as we have said, until recently neither an interculturally-based site nor practice have existed within the EM. The EM as initially constructed, needing to be built entirely upon validated interventions (either by gold-standard RCTs or by Expert Reference Group: two high, but different standards, of validation) left out attention to culture explicitly directed through any of its interventions. The fact, in itself, that neither the NICE survey nor the ERG one found a "best practice"—at the very least, intervention that focused upon intercultural issues—is a sad comment on our dominant culture's myopia.

So, jettisoning the need to have a model that conforms to the absolute highest standards of research practice was an inevitable outcome for the next phase of development of the EM. Otherwise we could not keep the EM in line with either attention to the fact that we are a global community or with society's current societal needs—in particular in geographical areas in which there is high intercultural marriage and cohabitation. We wished to move it to a higher ethical standard of practice which would accord with those needs. Indeed, the authors believe that it is current "best practice" to include the multicultural dimension. What has been yielded is The IEM.

THE INTERCULTURAL EXETER MODEL

The IEM gives practitioners a systemic-behavioral way to focus on the cultural context of a couple's life, and a method to bring in this necessary focus of so many couples today.

This version of the EM, as in the original one, does not assume pathology within the interactions, nor make an assumption of pathology about the inherent difficulties in uniting different cultures. Instead, it assumes these differences are often unwitting but that they can maintain problems. It highlights the cultural differences so that they can be brought into focus. This is so couples can name and recognize and empathize with each other about the unique challenges that these differences bring. These reside within a cultural context in which there may be differing values and beliefs that bring about different expectations around behaviors within life together. They may also reflect variations within the couple's background and actual cultural conditions—for instance, around sociopolitical differences and economic inequality. It is imperative, given these potentially powerful differences, that therapists be able to help a couple unearth how they affect interactional processes.

However, it is also imperative that therapists know how to guard against the opposite problem of not attending, unearthing, and understanding: pathologizing—that is, to guard against assuming that whatever the problem is, it is always related to intercultural/interfaith differences.

THE INTERVENTIONS OF THE INTERCULTURAL EXETER MODEL

Many of the interventions that are made within the adapted EM to fit intercultural work utilize the original methods, but direct the therapists to asking specific questions, using them around culture. However, just as we ask "what is the presenting problem" so that we can clearly delineate the maintenance cycle of that problem (e.g., "depression" with "depressive symptoms" at the top of the maintenance cycle), the IEM explicitly starts with "what is an intercultural couple?" Is this couple one which is facing issues that arise or are colored by being from different cultures? Sometimes the couple self-define as "intercultural," and sometimes the answer to this question is obvious, at face validity: the couple clearly come from different cultures or faith. But sometimes the answer is not obvious: sometimes intercultural couples might appear to be from the same culture, but because an earlier, different, generation's very strong influence, for instance, has dominated in one member's upbringing but not the other's, a different culture is having a real but not necessarily clearly observable impact. Or sometimes having been raised even partially within a different country or education system, or coming from a stronger versus a weaker faith system within the families-of-origin, can mean there are not obvious but still very strong and active cultural differences playing out within a couple.

The central theme in interculturally influenced therapy is to create a shared meaning to the extent that it is possible, while tolerating the differences. To achieve this we use two particular interventions designed to address culture, but also we build questions from interventions within the EM to access cultural ideas and potential tensions or dilemmas.

These are such questions as what is the meaning of home, for instance, or the loss of home for displaced cultures; or the important but different and differently valued practices of religion and culture; or the beliefs of religion and culture associated with distress or mental health difficulties; or experiences of racism, disadvantage, and expectations of protection; or of differences in parenting styles and ways of relating to extended families. These are now, through the development of the intercultural part, specifically built into the extant EM interventions. For example, the IEM will be asking therapists to help couples explore what is the "script" around mental health or their present distress, within each of the cultures, or, while designing a family genogram the therapist will be asking about such things.

But in addition to building specificity within the existing interventions, there are two specifically culturally focused methods that we also use. These are discussed in the following sections.

THE CULTURAL GENOGRAM: A KEY INTERVENTION

The cultural genogram (Hardy & Laszloffy, 1995) enquires about the cultural, ethnic, and religious heritages of the people *explicitly* within the genogram. Within intercultural work, this is "best practice" intervention and as such it has become a key intervention within the IEM.

The cultural genogram is a method to expand the couple's stories and ability to question their often unspoken differing and potentially conflictual cultural practices and beliefs. Via cultural genograms partners can discuss their cultural backgrounds, recount beliefs carried by family members in generations past, and convey their feelings regarding family rituals and legacies. Genograms are also an opportunity to bring into view contradictions among historical narratives originating both in each partner's family of origin and in the larger society (i.e., what is discussed and what has been omitted, and by whom and for what purposes). Specific family themes, such as heterogamous relationships, cultural ancestry, and the circumstances under which partners' ancestors entered the country can be coded with colors and/or symbols that carry meaning for each partner. Family photographs, cultural artifacts, and recreating a cultural ritual in the therapy room can add to the experience (Hardy & Laszloffy, 1995; Singh, Killian, Bhugun, & Tseng, 2020).

The cultural genogram can be used in conjunction with the EM method of tracking the maintenance cycle of the interacting circularities: the thoughts and feelings part of which may well be informed by these differing yet unspoken beliefs and assumed practices. Vicious cycles have the possibilities to become virtuous cycles: adding in explicitly the intercultural dimension can unearth deeply held ideas and expectations that can block this process if not made clear.

The method for doing this is the cultural genogram, an illustration of which will appear in the second part of this book.

THE CULTUREGRAM: A SECOND INTERCULTURAL METHOD OF INTERVENTION

The culturegram is an assessment tool that originates in Berlin and Cannon's (2013) work. Together the therapist and clients construct a diagram that provides a chance for intercultural couples to do some thinking about the differences in their family beliefs, values, traditions, and legacies. It charts beliefs and values that affect the couple's lives that may or may not be unconsciously directing them around particularly meaningful and often divisive areas of their lives. The themes can vary, for instance, from religious values to ideas about sex, to disciplining children to education, to gender roles, to ideas about work and home life.

Through exploring specific themes, chosen by the couple, within the diagram, families' similarities and differences are laid bare and clarified. The diagram comprises a series of circles that depict beliefs and practices of their respective families, with linking lines to how they play out within their present relationship.

A fuller description and illustration of the culturegram and an example of its use is in the second part of the book.

WHO CAN USE THE INTERCULTURAL EXETER MODEL?

Therapists who have worked within either the systemic or behavioral models who work with couples would be able to work within the systemic-behavioral model. Indeed, trainees in the original model were drawn from both of these groups. For systemically trained therapists it trains in the use and rationale for validated practices of CBT within the conceptual framework of systemic practice. For CBT trained practitioners it gives a way to think and practice within the context of interactions and the larger framework of their clients' lives. For those trained in both ways of working it gives an integrated rationale for combining techniques.

THE FORMAT OF THE BOOK

The model is manualized, as set forth in the second part of this book, and so, for therapists, working to specific interventions that are clearly defined, this means it affords clarity about the use of these largely validated and endorsed interventions and a framework for why they are deployed. This is usual practice within CBT, as is specifying what the presenting problem the work is targeting, and agreeing to this—which the IEM maintenance cycle work does. However these are not necessarily an expected part of normal practice for systemic therapists. We think that this idea of the maintenance cycle helps to guide the therapist toward clearer, more accountable and collaborative work, and, for the client, it promotes clarity in communication both with the therapist and the other member of the couple. (For example, from the beginning what they are working on has been stated and agreed upon.) Finally, the EM in both of its versions—the EM and the IEM—specifies largely validated interventions that will guide the therapy.

The first part of this book describes and situates the development of the model in broad terms. The second part shows the interventions of the model, describing the intervention first, then showing it in action in script form. This shows the work in action with two specific, intercultural couples.

CHAPTER 2

The Wider Context of the Intercultural Exeter Model

Systemic practice shows the importance of contextualizing what we see. And to understand the "why" of the IEM, the emergence of the original model within a sea of politics is critical. Those politics were both national and local to the university in which it was housed, each sea flowing into and out of one another.

The first and bigger one, that of the UK's political climate, increasingly has meant a demand for a solid research evidence base for treatment funding. This is true both for strictly medical regimes and for psychological therapies. Because there is a National Health Service, the UK's main health provider, this quite rightly and expectedly means there is a tight watch on expenditure, which means a very reasonable demand for an evidence base for treatments. Since the beginning of this century it became increasingly clear that a large part of the health budget—including visits to and consequent treatments by GPs, as well as the use of NHS hospital services—was from sufferers of depression. In consequence there was a large national impetus to establish best practice—that is, best evidence for treatment—to treat depression. It is this wider politically based demand and effort that formed part of the genesis of the EM.

A byproduct of the emphasis on establishing an evidence base for psychological and medical treatment procurement, in general, is the salience of NICE—the National Institute of Clinical Excellence—in which the best available scientific evidence for treatments is collated by experts in their respective fields. NICE then makes recommendations based on this collation. The "best available" equates to "gold standard" researched treatments: randomly controlled research trials to establish a therapy's or medicine's effectiveness. This is inarguably crucial in the case of drugs and other strictly medical interventions (we would most wish to take a drug that is certainly, rather than "maybe, possibly, we think" effective). Treatments for depression were assessed by NICE to establish this "gold standard" for recommended practice.

The Intercultural Exeter Couples Model: Making Connections for a Divided World Through Systemic-Behavioral Therapy, First Edition. Janet Reibstein and Reenee Singh.
© 2021 John Wiley & Sons Ltd. Published 2021 by John Wiley & Sons Ltd.

But to employ the gold standard to psychotherapy—in this case for depression—can be problematic. Conducting RCTs can take years: to get research funding, or to set up the proper control conditions—for example, getting the variables under study well matched with control conditions—can be both tricky and cumbersome. And—maybe the most difficult—defining the variables clearly to show that they, and not something else, are the reasons for a treatment's effectiveness—can be challenging and often elusive.

Partly for this reason the "gold standard" studies cited by NICE within psychotherapy for depression, and in the particular case concerning the interest of the IEM, (couples therapy), particularly up to and through the 1990s, have been on behavioral therapy (BT). It is much easier to pinpoint, and therefore, define a behavior you ask someone to do (for instance, to use a statement that starts with "I feel" rather than "you always do," say, than to define a therapeutic intervention which asks someone to do something more amorphous and abstract, for instance, to attempt to make a "transferential interpretation.") Crucially also for systemic practitioners, it is also the case that looking at discrete behaviors is a lot easier than looking at the "context" in which they occur. How do we define the relevant aspects of a family or couple's context? Where do we stop—at the level of the household, of the neighborhood, of the family heritage? And what are the best ways to define these, even so—so that if we have a control condition to ensure we are solely investigating the influence of our systemic treatment—how are we going to set up the right controls?

So, in the end, behavioral therapies are, in general, the ones that gain the gold star. Indeed, these continue to be the ones that NICE recommends, and so, begins a reifying process: the type of research that has been done and approved of is the type of research that is likely to keep being funded. CBT (Cognitive Behavioral Therapy)—the inheritor of BT—is more likely to be funded, more likely to be the therapy of choice for clinical researchers, than others, and others are less likely to be funded in a major way, as a result. The more a treatment is validated, the more likely further ones will be funded. This is where the sea of university politics begins.

The discourse within the politics of mental health continues to vaunt the "evidence-based, gold standard" modalities, to the disadvantage of other ones. Most research is done within universities. In the field of couples therapy, behavioral couples therapy research, much of it done, of course, in the 1970s, 1980s, and 1990s, was able to publish results of RCTs establishing effectiveness in treating depression. Most of it came out of universities.

However, because it takes a long time for studies both to get set up (i.e., funding, careful execution of the research) and then to be published, these studies are often out of date with current practice, which moves on and on. The political sea is one of "evidence-based practice." But the treatment one is of "practice-based evidence." If it seems to be effective it carries on. Indeed, there is other, less than "gold" standard research carried on: there is "face validity" to the effectiveness of some of the more difficult interventions (for instance, "creating a safe space" and "exploring family script issues"—both of which are EM interventions); there is anecdotal or "seeming" evidence from feedback from clients, therapists, and supervisors (although this is, of course, not solid); and there are more formal audits that ask about symptom reduction and satisfaction or other outcome variables, that support new practices.

So, in 2009 NICE recommended, among other treatments for depression, "behavioral couples therapy." Here is the introductory statement by NICE in its guidelines.

> A time-limited, psychological intervention derived from a model of the interactional processes in relationships where the intervention aims to help participants understand the effects of their interactions on each other as factors in the development and/or maintenance of symptoms and problems. The aim is to change the nature of the interactions so that they may develop more supportive and less conflictual relationships.
>
> (National Institute of Clinical Excellence [NICE], 2009)

What followed was a list of behaviorally based separate interventions culled from six gold standard behavioral couples treatment studies, such as "making I statements" or "homework tasks."

But partly as a consequence of acknowledgment of the problem of exclusively recommending interventions that could be out of date and narrow, the UK government initiated, in the mid-noughties, a series of "Expert Reference Groups" (ERGs), across the myriad of therapeutic modalities, beginning with CBT, continuing on to Systemic and Psychodynamic, then to Humanistic, to Couples Therapy, and so on. These groups, comprising nominated experts in each of these modalities, were to come to an agreement on best practice currently in use. The first author (JR) was a member of the ERG on systemic practice, and advisor to the ERG on couples therapy (to ensure a systemic voice was given to this enterprise). The second author (RS) was a member of a group, founded and facilitated by Eia Asen, which reviewed the competencies recommended by the ERG. Added to the NICE behavioral interventions (gold standard) were the "practice-based evidence"—or current best practice interventions—agreed upon by these groups.

The other political context, to which we have alluded, was that of the universities, and in particular the university in which JR was Professor of Psychology, the University of Exeter. In the midst of these developments for treating depression, the University of Exeter offered an opportunity for systemically informed practice to become more researchable, once NICE had recommended "behavioural couples therapy as a treatment for depression."

A university-based research and training clinic, supported by the NHS but housed within the university, was set up. Research and clinical psychology and systemic therapy students would work in it. The politics of the university, vaunting establishing evidence base within a research lab or clinic, meant that the brief for the clinic was that the treatments within it had to conform to NICE guidelines, but also be innovative so that new, viable types of treatment could be researched. This was a gauntlet set down.

The task was to argue that there is a "behavioral couples therapy" treatment that could be situated within a systemic framework, and with a commonly agreed-upon, if not entirely gold-standard, validated set of interventions. In order to establish the validity and potential effectiveness of such a new treatment modality—one that is both behavioral and evidentially systemic—a systematic, manualized set of practices needed to be devised, one that would teach clinical trainees clearly and also provide the possibility of researching the treatment, itself. The challenge was both to establish a clinic and also to write a manual for it.

This is where JR's experience on both the UK government's ERGs came into play. As a systemic overseer of the couples ERG, to ensure that there was a systemic perspective, she was able to see which competencies, or best practice interventions, were within a clearly acceptable systemic set of practices. As a clinically trained psychologist who has worked behaviorally (as well as psychodynamically) she could ascertain which of the behavioral interventions fit within a systemic tradition of practice and as a systemically trained practitioner to see how to fit them into a systemic framework. With her colleague, Hannah Sherbersky (HS) at the University of Exeter, she devised a manual of such interventions within a systemic rationale, for use within a training and research clinic, and a case was made to include this in the university clinic, which already was providing treatment within a range of behaviorally based group and individual modalities. In 2011 the EM treatment was launched within the University of Exeter AccEPT clinic, with JR and HS running and supervising it.

Here is where a different strand of research becomes relevant, that of the two behavioral couples therapy clinicians and researchers referred to in Chapter 1, Jacobson and Christenson (1998) whose research at that point questioned the durability of treatment effectiveness of simple behavioral couples therapy. Their research established a short effectiveness span of about 6 months for simple behavioral couples therapy, after which the treatment's effects wore off. They themselves had been early advocates of behavioral couples therapy but felt that what was lacking were the elements of what they termed "acceptance" and "tolerance." That is, they concluded, to make changes longer-lasting, people needed to place their learned behavioral change within an understanding of their partner's needs and feelings and to have that reciprocated. They found that couples could learn new behaviors.

But these new behaviors tailed off unless they had an understanding of and empathy for the reasons for these changes. They also needed to understand and accept their own and their partner's tolerance levels for each behavioral change. Jacobson and Christensen added in interventions that they termed "acceptance" and "tolerance" interventions in their therapy, did further research, and found that treatment effects were much longer lasting if these were also part of the therapy.

The ERG best practice interventions did, in fact, include a set of interventions that could be seen as falling within the rubric of "acceptance" and "tolerance." They included many that other therapies have described and prioritized, such as Emotionally Focused Couples Therapy (EFCT), but also many more traditional therapies, including psychodynamic and systemic couple modalities.

These interventions, all within a broad behavioral couples frame (now including more than behavioral interventions), in the formulation of NICE, can each, separately and together, be used to try to disrupt the patterns of interactions that are maintaining the symptoms of depression. There is no theoretical frame for this recommended approach, apart from the systemically informed proposition contained within the NICE recommendation that recommends an "… intervention aims to help participants understand the effects of their interactions on each other as factors in the development and/or maintenance of symptoms and problems." (NICE, 2009). However, this statement, in itself, makes it a systemically informed treatment.

The EM/IEM categorize the agreed upon, validated (either by NICE or ERG) interventions as "behavioral" and "empathic"—the "empathic" ones fit Jacobson and Christensen's acceptance and tolerance category. All of the interventions are ones the ERG identified, and all are within acceptable and normal systemic practice (others that are not, such as ones that are clearly within a psychodynamic framework that, for instance, refer to the workings of the transference, are not included, as they would not be systemic).

In this sense, the EM is a "behavioral/systemic" one. Its interventions would be familiar to a systemically trained practitioner. Its behavioral ones, but not its non-behavioral ones necessarily, would be familiar to a CBT practitioner. However, putting these together in a logically coherent way remained a challenge and one that begged to be made rather than have an approach that was simply a collection of parts.

This is where, for the first author, a profound truism established within the research of Gottman (1994) became a pivotal feature of the EM/IEM. In his research Gottman found, by noting the minute-to-minute interactions, over long chunks of time periods (he installed cameras in his "Love Lab" house in which couples resided for weekends), that couples' satisfying versus unsatisfying, as well as stable versus unstable, relationships could be identified by how each member responded to the other. That could be positively or negatively, in a build-up, over time, of moment-to-moment interactions. Yet these are hardly noticeable by people, even though these together form the sum total of their feelings about each other, about themselves in relation to the other, and about the relationship, in general. How good the relationship is lies in these minute interchanges. Thus, a conclusion is that the power to change the quality can lie there: changing these minute inter-actions. Interventions focus on the feedback loop of such interactions that have maintained the symptom that is causing malfunctioning within the couple—and in the case of depression, this can been either wittingly or unwittingly so. For instance in the case of very loving or caring couples their interactions may have yielded a sense of helplessness or a sense of uselessness or guilt in the depressed one that have "helped" the depression to survive. That build-up of minute interactions in a feedback cycle is key to keeping the depression (or any problematic situation) going. So, as in the NICE recommendations, interrupting that usual pattern of interactions with new behaviors can be the key to stopping it, and thus forms the basis of couples therapy treatment. We are talking here about feedback loops; however, this time, if we follow in Gottman's footsteps, these are loops built up of tiny moments, with the key to change lying in painstakingly breaking these down.

Systemic practice, indeed, focuses on feedback loops of interactions—how one person does something that produces a response in the other, and then a response in return, etc. But more often than not such loops are explored in large swoops—one person "does" X, another "does" Y in response, and so on. More often than not these "doings" are often conflated with "feelings" or "thoughts." So-and-so gets angry; this leads to the partner of so-and-so feeling bad, which leads to so-and-so closing down, which leads to the partner thinking she's been a bad girl, which leads to so-and-so being aggressive. These are thoughts, feelings, and behaviors conflated, and the sequence is unclear—what and why did so-and-so do that made his partner think he was angry in the first place, for example? How is this couple able to pin down exactly how, when, and why to change this cycle? Moreover, the accuracy of these responses that the couple reports—that is, whether the member of the couple is right about his or her reaction, or the feeling he or she has accurately reflected what the other person's behavior actually meant, not to mention the "why" of each person's response or feeling or thought—remain unexplored.

CBT also looks at feedback loops, but these loops are individual and internal: a particular thought can, indeed, bring on a behavior, which can bring on a feeling, or a thought or a behavior, all in response to each other, reinforcing each other—or this can occur in any order. Each of these of course reinforce the other, in a feedback loop.

CBT's loop has brought in a level that systemic hasn't in its general practice deconstructed usefully—that of thoughts, feelings, and behavior within those individuals within the systemically defined feedback loop. And systemic has brought in a dimension of reinforcement of behavior seen by CBT therapists that these therapists have left out—that of the input from and response to the other—the interactional aspect—and its reinforcing power.

The IEM has put these together, in a uniquely combined circularity, or feedback loop. In doing so, it also draws on a theoretical model of human behavior from a post-modernist position, Coordinated Management of Meaning (CMM) (Pearce, 2007). For it is entirely possible to read Gottman's findings on couple satisfaction and endurance in terms of the "meanings" each member of the couple gives to the responses given to them—whether positive or negative—by the other. A balance of mostly negative responses builds to a narrative of a negative relationship, fuelled by resentment and negative attributions of motives that help give a cohesive negative form to that narrative. A balance of mostly positive ones over time builds to a cohesively positive narrative, in which positive attributions are given (he or she is "tired" rather than he or she is "selfish," for instance, if something goes awry between them).

In Chapter 3 we expand on this CBT/Systemic Couples Maintenance Cycle that is the fulcrum of the IEM method.

The Fulcrum of the Method

The CBT/Systemic Couples Maintenance Cycle

The EM circularity posits that an emblematic episode, as in Pearce and Cronen's CMM (Pearce & Cronen, 1980), can be a window to the "meanings" that each person gives to it, drawing on their past history together to do so (when other instances like it have occurred); drawing on the meanings given to things from their respective family histories or scripts (for instance, ideas of what is "expectable" behavior from spouses in the sort of episode occurring); and drawing on their respective cultures, religions, ethnicities, and historical time periods (ditto).

The IEM also posits that people make assumptions and attributions about things based on these histories and often do not check them out to see if they are making the right meaning of them for the other person; moreover, unless they make their perceptions or their meanings explicit, they base these only on observed behavior—though they make assumptions about the thoughts and feelings behind the behavior: they only see behavior (or lack of it—silence and stasis are as powerful as their opposites). And they draw conclusions about meaning (what the thoughts and feelings must be) from what they observe. But these meanings may be wrong and distorted. This would be especially so if and when there is negative feeling within the couple or there has been a narrative built up that is largely so. By and large most of our interactions do not need to be explicated, and in good relationships in which there is much sympathy and empathy—which would also mean more positive interactions—the assumptions of the thoughts and feelings behind behaviors are often accurate. In disengaged, and less well functioning relationships (the sum of interactions is more negative) these are often not accurate. These cry out for breaking the moment-to-moment loops down so that shared meanings, more accurate understandings, can occur.

The Intercultural Exeter Couples Model: Making Connections for a Divided World Through Systemic-Behavioral Therapy, First Edition. Janet Reibstein and Reenee Singh.
© 2021 John Wiley & Sons Ltd. Published 2021 by John Wiley & Sons Ltd.

THE INTERCULTURAL EXETER MODEL CIRCULARITY: A CBT/SYSTEMIC INTERVENTION

So, the IEM circularity, in which the systemic-behavioral interventions are defined, with an example, takes a chosen episode, emblematic of typical ways of interacting, that ends up maintaining depression, for instance, or whatever it is that has brought a couple into therapy. It breaks it down into a feedback loop of moment-to-moment interactions in which there are thoughts, feelings, and behaviors for each partner at each moment. Only the behaviors are usually apparent. So it starts, as in the usual systemic way, asking what behavior on the part of one happens and then what behavior on the part of the other was in response, etc. all the way around through a day that ended up maintaining the problem (defined through thoughts, feelings, and behavior on the part of the problematic person or persons).

As in CMM it starts with the couple naming a prototypical episode. This is then charted, moment-to-moment: it links, in a feedback loop of responses, each member's *behavior* that is observed by the other, in response to each other, on and on, until what is shown is that those behaviors are maintaining the behavior that is the symptom of the presenting problem (at the top of the cycle). Then it goes back over the cycle which has described the observable behaviors, and asks each couple member to describe what their *thoughts and feelings* were at each of those points—that is, the non-observables. It shows how the one's *behavior* (the observable or audible behavior, itself, only) brings a reaction from the other (this can include silence or apparent non-reaction: it is what is observed or heard by the other that is important) and then what reaction (*behavior*) on the first person this second person's observed behavior has upon the second, and so on, in sequence till at the top of the cycle you see how the depression, which was already there at the beginning of the cycle, is being (usually unwittingly) maintained by the couple's behavioral interactional cycle. Then, in this cycle the therapist goes back and asks each partner, as she goes through the cycle of behaviors, to add in the thoughts and feelings at each of these behavior points in the sequence of the cycle. This usually is a revelation when either what they'd each thought the other meant by his or her behavior was not at all what they'd thought or that it was just a bit different, and often different in a surprising and enlightening way.

The idea is that if these tacit things were made explicit, in many cases it could and would change the other's assumptions and attributions they've given, often erroneously, to the meanings of the observed behavior. Now there would be no—often erroneous—guesswork. They would learn what their partner actually thought and felt and what perhaps erroneous sense they might have been making about each behavior at each moment, or point in the cycle, that they had been observing. And the same would be true for their partner, in turn.

Once the correct information is in the open, it offers numerous pathways to change. It offers opportunities for the therapist to bring in the other IEM interventions to help guide the change in a positive direction. It gives the couple the opportunity to reflect on themselves and each other, to learn about each other and to gain the empathic understanding that taking away incorrect, often undermining assumptions can block. It gives, finally, through much of these, pathways to different sorts of relating and understanding, and the couple the chance, through guided work with the IEM interventions, to make different choices of behavior at similar moments, when they arise again between them.

This circularity forms the basis for then bringing in the other interventions in the IEM. We will show this in action in the next part of the book, when we identify the interventions of the IEM. Describing the *couple's maintenance cycle*, itself, can be the focus of change and disruption through the revelations about meanings it evokes; can form the basis of where the couple can choose to act or react differently, to "disrupt" the maintenance cycle; and it also acts as a basis for opening windows into other important potentially therapeutic moments. At each point in the cycle, as you take the couple through it, one of the other of the interventions can be brought in.

For instance, in order to investigate why someone might assume that their partner must be feeling in a certain way for them to behave in the way observed, questions could be asked not only about the history of the couple's interactions, but also about their *culturally based* family scripts about such incidents or behavior. In these numerous opportunities for them to change their behaviors, thereupon, within the maintenance cycle can occur. This means not only increasing understandings, empathic connections, and new behavior repertoires, but in the end, creating new circularities that do not maintain the symptom (depression, in this case, but also any other, in theory, being treated), and therefore, treating the reason for coming into therapy in the first place. In this way, the IEM, in theory, can be effective.

The two diagrams in the following sections show the IEM circularity, in the couple cases we will see in Part 2, described below. In the next chapter we describe each of these separate interventions. And in the following one(s) we take these model couple cases within parts of hypothetical therapy sessions.

Helen and Rebecca Circularity

This circularity—which keeps the couple in a state of discord and disengagement—shows how the observed behaviors, explicit and implicit—keep this going; assumptions are made by each about the motivations and probable feelings and intentions behind the observed responses to them, respectively. But these are often wrong and lead then to badly judged responses, which become the observed explicit or implicit behaviors by the next person receiving it, who also then makes assumptions that could be wrong, and so on. The following circularities show how the discord and disengagement between Rebecca and Helen are maintained by each one's response to the other, and how the depression and consequent disengagement as well are maintained by the same process in the case of Raja and Fiona. The unsaid, hidden thoughts and feelings, if unearthed, could lead to changes in the way each one understands the other and how the responses could be different.

Helen and Rebecca begin from a state of discord/disengagement, as seen in the first behavior we choose for the circularity. The final behavior, as we shall see, maintains this state, and so feeds back to it, in a circular way. An arrow from that last behavior, indicating this, would lead straight back to this first one, showing how it is all being maintained.

REMEMBER: Thoughts and feelings in each of the pieces of the circularity are NOT observed, and so remain UNKNOWN.

Helen: Behavior: "Rebecca, you've left the cap off the toothpaste off again."

Thoughts: Why on earth is Rebecca so messy? Why do I have to live in such a messy, chaotic environment? I know she comes from that liberal, Israeli, let it all hang out way of life! It's coming out even in the fact she can't remember to clean up after herself in the bathroom, for goodness sake! And she thinks it's my uptight Britishness that is the reason I go on at her, I just know it.

Feelings: Anger, resentment.

This *behavior*, observed, of Helen's leads to Rebecca's *behavior in response* to her:

Rebecca: Behavior (in response to Helen's observed behavior to her): "Please let me sleep—it's too early in the morning to wake up."

Thoughts: Here she goes again, so anal! It is just so uptight. So unfeeling. So British!

Feelings: Fear—Helen is going to get angry with me now and ruin my morning. Anger—Why do I have to wake up to this shouting every day? Why do I have to wake up so early?

This *behavior*, observed, in turn, of Rebecca's leads to Helen's *behavior in response* to her:

Helen: Behavior (in response to Rebecca's behavior to her): "How come you're always asleep? If only you would wake up earlier, you would have enough time to study, and to tidy up at the end of the day."

Thoughts: Why is Rebecca so lazy? She doesn't have any of the right values that we have in our family/our culture/religion—they just used to let her do and say whatever she wanted to, as if that's the highest value, and not respecting others, being considerate, at all.

Feelings: Indignation, resentment at being the only one to wake up early and to tidy up.

This *behavior*, observed, in turn, of Helen's leads to Rebecca's *behavior in response* to her:

Rebecca: Behavior (in response to Helen's observed behavior to her): "That's it. I'm not going to listen to any of your crap first thing in the morning. I need to sleep." (Picks up her pillow and duvet and leaves the room to go and sleep in the guest room.)

Thoughts: I have to get away from this tirade. She thinks it's so important when it's more important to chill out and let people have a little freedom. Rules about this and that—for god's sake, this whole country needs to lighten up!

Feelings: Panic and a need to escape.

This *behavior*, observed, in turn, of Rebecca's leads to Helen's *behavior in response* to her:

Helen: Behavior (in response to Rebecca's behavior to her): She pursues Rebecca out of the room. "Rebecca, will you at least put the cap back on the toothpaste!"

Thoughts: If I don't chase her and get her to listen to me, I will spend all my time picking up after her and live in the kind of chaos and emotional diarrhea I see in all her family and they think is fine!

Feelings: Fury, rage.

This *behavior*, observed, in turn, of Helen's leads to Rebecca's *behavior in response* to her:

Rebecca: Behavior: Slams door in Helen's face.

Thoughts: She needs to be stopped—she's like a dictator!

Feelings: I feel trapped and stifled and I am furious and also sad.

This *behavior*, observed, in turn, of Rebecca's leads to Helen's *behavior in response* to her:

Helen: Behavior: Leaves the house.

Thoughts: She is uncontrollable—a slob and a child.

Feelings: I am furious and also sad.

This *behavior*, observed, in turn, of Helen's leads to Rebecca's *behavior in response* to her.

She, for instance, does not care about leaving the cap of the toothpaste off, not caring that it bothers Helen, doesn't get out of bed, not caring that

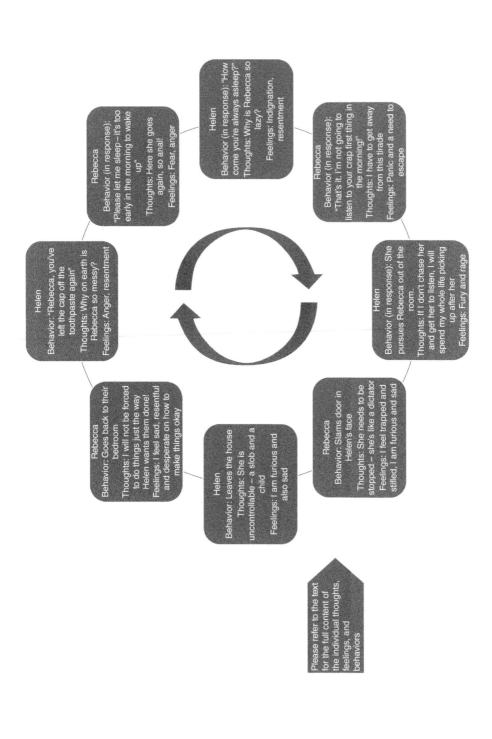

Helen
Behavior (in response): "How come you're always asleep?"
Thoughts: Why is Rebecca so lazy?
Feelings: Indignation, resentment

Rebecca
Behavior (in response): "Please let me sleep—it's too early in the morning to wake up"
Thoughts: Here she goes again, so anal!
Feelings: Fear, anger

Rebecca
Behavior (in response): "That's it, I'm not going to listen to your crap first thing in the morning!"
Thoughts: I have to get away from this tirade
Feelings: Panic and a need to escape

Helen
Behavior: "Rebecca, you've left the cap off the toothpaste again"
Thoughts: Why on earth is Rebecca so messy?
Feelings: Anger, resentment

Helen
Behavior (in response): She pursues Rebecca out of the room.
Thoughts: If I don't chase her and get her to listen, I will spend my whole life picking up after her
Feelings: Fury and rage

Rebecca
Behavior: Goes back to their bedroom
Thoughts: I will not be forced to do things just the way Helen wants them done!
Feelings: I feel sad, resentful and desperate on how to make things okay

Rebecca
Behavior: Slams door in Helen's face
Thoughts: She needs to be stopped – she's like a dictator
Feelings: I feel trapped and stifled, I am furious and sad

Helen
Behavior: Leaves the house
Thoughts: She is uncontrollable – a slob and a child
Feelings: I am furious and also sad

Please refer to the text for the full content of the individual thoughts, feelings, and behaviors it bothers Helen, and then Helen will, or could, rage again about the same thing—or another like it. And so on and so on, in a circular fashion.

What is being maintained is their estrangement from each other, by the act of slamming, finally, on the one hand, and leaving, on the other, as well as their division from each other of understanding their differences, and their sadness and anger at not being able to be as loving as they would like to be and sometimes can be, toward each other.

Fiona and Raja Circularity

(It is morning and the alarm goes off for both of the couple to get out of bed.)

We start with depressive behavior which gets maintained, as well as the disengagement that goes with it as a result of their behaviors and responses to each other.

Fiona:	Behavior: Turns over, pulls sheet and blanket over her head and begins to breathe heavily.
Thoughts:	I can't face getting up. I am not ready to go back to work yet and I can't face the day. I know Raja is going to blame me, think I'm useless, and I want him to hold me and tell me I'm okay but I know he doesn't think I am so he won't, so I'm going to turn over so I don't have to face him either. He thinks I am "sick" like his mother was when he was a kid and she was in bed. He doesn't "get" it! I am sick, anyway. I am useless and more useless because I am "sick"! I just want to sleep these useless feelings away.
Feelings:	Useless, depressed, sad, yearning for reassurance.

This *behavior* from Fiona leads to Raja's *response in behavior* to her:

Raja:	Behavior: (Notices Fiona turning over and pulling the blankets over her as he gets out of bed): Sighs. Thinks about saying something. Gets out of bed and doesn't say anything. Creeps into bathroom to get ready, tiptoeing, and leaves, after getting ready, without saying goodbye.
Thoughts:	I don't know what to do when she's like this. She's ill; it's best to let her sleep, that's what I learned growing up. She's got an "illness"—that's what the doctors say but she doesn't seem to be getting better, although I don't see what else I could do. I hope she gets better soon because this is going on for far too long. At least I can carry on getting to work!
Feelings:	Impatience, hopelessness, uselessness.

This *behavior* from Raja leads to Fiona's *response in behavior* to him:

Fiona: Behavior: Lies in bed, not sleeping, tossing and turning. Stays in bed for the rest of the day. Turns off phone.

Thoughts: I'm turning off my phone—that will show him! How can he just leave me like that without asking how I am or trying to get me up? How can he not be concerned that I am still in bed? He just doesn't care. And he doesn't because I am useless. He must be resenting me—he thinks it's so important to "achieve" and earn, like they all do in his family and I can't even get out of bed to work and get a job. And I'm just like my mother. Useless, unable to work.

Feelings: Anger at Raja for leaving, but sadness, depression, sadness, uselessness.

This *behavior* from Fiona leads to Raja's *response in behavior* to her:

Raja: Behavior (at work): Texts her without response on and off all day. Then goes home careful not to disturb her, observing she is still in bed, and creeps into bed without speaking.

Thoughts: What's the matter with her phone? What's the matter with her? Is it that she feels so sick that she doesn't want to be disturbed? I am worried that I can't reach her. But maybe she's trying to prove something to me; maybe she doesn't want me. Maybe I'm not doing what she wants me to do. Her family is such a mess and her mother was, she says, sick like this, but I don't think they know what to do either. But as she's "ill" I think I'll just leave her alone.

Feelings: Frustration, concern, worry, uselessness.

This *behavior* from Raja leads to Fiona's *response in behavior* to him. She stays in bed, feeling useless, more depressed, and he keeps his distance. The next morning is likely to breed the same or similar behavior from Fiona, in response to Raja's end of day behavior from him, as above, in a circular fashion.

What is being maintained in this couple is their feelings of uselessness, respectively, Fiona's depression, and their mutual separation from the support and reassurance and loving connection each one needs as a result of Fiona's depression on their move to a new city and loss of a job. They maintain their divided understanding of the condition of depression and what to do as a result of it that, instead, could be "supportive."

In the next chapter we discuss the other pole of the IEM: the intercultural themes in such couples work.

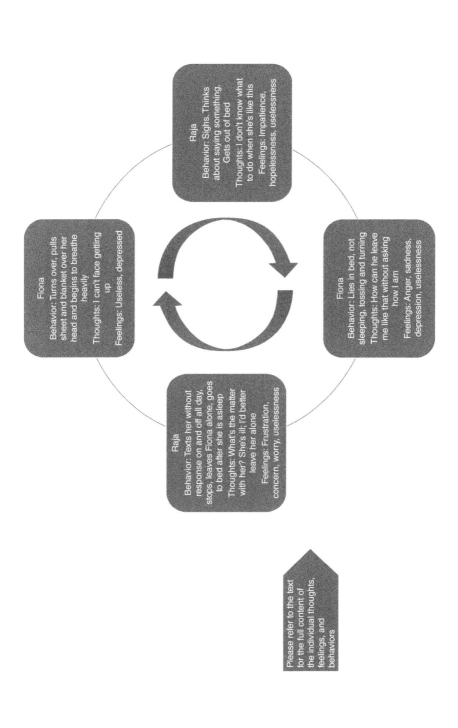

Raja
Behavior: Sighs. Thinks about saying something. Gets out of bed
Thoughts: I don't know what to do when she's like this
Feelings: Impatience, hopelessness, uselessness

Fiona
Behavior: Turns over, pulls sheet and blanket over her head and begins to breathe heavily
Thoughts: I can't face getting up
Feelings: Useless, depressed

Fiona
Behavior: Lies in bed, not sleeping, tossing and turning
Thoughts: How can he leave me like that without asking how I am
Feelings: Anger, sadness, depression, uselessness

Raja
Behavior: Texts her without response on and off all day, stops, leaves Fiona alone, goes to bed after she is asleep
Thoughts: What's the matter with her? She's ill; I'd better leave her alone
Feelings: Frustration, concern, worry, uselessness

Please refer to the text for the full content of the individual thoughts, feelings, and behaviors

CHAPTER 4

Clinical Practice with Intercultural Couples

Themes and Processes

The growth of immigration, changes in social mores and expectations, and advances in global technology have contributed to an increase in intercultural marriages and relationships worldwide, including interracial, interfaith, interethnic, and international partnerships (Bhugun, 2017). In the United Kingdom alone, 2.3 million people are living with or married to somebody from a different ethnic group, and 1 in 10 relationships are intercultural. The figures for London are even higher, and it is predicted that by 2030 50% of people living there will be foreign-born (2011 Census), which will increase the number of intercultural intimate relationships. In the United States, almost 4 in 10 Americans (39%) who have married since 2010 have married those from different religious groups (Murphy, 2015). In the UK one might hypothesize that if 1 in 10 relationships in England and Wales is between people of two different ethnic/cultural groups it is likely that many of these will be interfaith relationships (Singh, 2017).

The term "intercultural" encompasses the different notions of ethnic, interethnic, racial, interracial, religious, interfaith, and country of birth. In the Western literature on intercultural couples the term "intercultural" refers to the interactions between members of different cultural groups (Ting-Toomey, 1999). An intercultural couple is regarded as two adults in a relationship who have significant differences in nationalities, race, religion, ethnicity, and language (McFadden & Moore, 2001; Perel, 2000; Sullivan & Cottone, 2006). However, intercultural relationships carry different meanings across cultures and contexts. For example, in India "intercultural" refers to relationships in which the partners come from different caste backgrounds and communities. In other countries partners might identify as "intercultural" if they come from different class backgrounds, or if they are from the

The Intercultural Exeter Couples Model: Making Connections for a Divided World Through Systemic-Behavioral Therapy, First Edition. Janet Reibstein and Reenee Singh.
© 2021 John Wiley & Sons Ltd. Published 2021 by John Wiley & Sons Ltd.

same ethnic background but grew up in different countries. Similarly, couples from the same religious background may identify as "intercultural" because of the difference in the strength of their religious beliefs. In some countries or cultures unions between those of different faiths are considered "intercultural," while in others, different class backgrounds or political values and beliefs, constitute "cultural differences." Here, the notion of *intersectionality* (the intersection of different identities) is important, as sometimes differences might go hand in hand and at other times similarity at one level, for example, social class, might override other racial and cultural differences (Singh, Killian, Bhugun, & Tseng, 2020).

When we refer to "intercultural couples," we are describing both heterosexual and gay and lesbian couples, whilst acknowledging that gay and lesbian couples may have additional specific issues around intersectionality. Further, same-sex couples tend to have intercultural relationships in higher numbers than straight couples. An analysis of the 2010 U.S. Census data (Queer Voices, 2016) found that 20.6% of same-sex couples were interracial or interethnic, compared to 18.3% of straight unmarried couples and 9.5% of straight married couples.

OVERVIEW

Until recently, the literature on intercultural relationships focused on psychosocial challenges, such as barriers to communication (Perel, 2000; Waldman & Rubalcava, 2005), conflicts over parenting (Ho, 1990; Romano, 2001), and differences in cultural values, (Garcia, 2006; Hsu, 2001; Waldman & Rubalcava, 2005). According to Cadenhead (2018), the unique stressors intercultural couples face have received significant attention, with researchers focusing on contrasting religious affiliations and cultural values (Nabeshima, 2005), relationships with extended family (Seshadri & Knudson-Martin, 2013), cultural differences in communication (Herr, 2009; Llerena-Quinn & Bacigalupe, 2009; Sprenkle, Davis, & Lebow, 2009) and childrearing responsibilities (Romano, 1988). Another area of research has been the role of power dynamics in intercultural couples and how power is mediated through differences in language, race, and gender (Bystydzienski, 2011; Molina et al., 2004). Marital satisfaction has also been linked to the successful acculturation of the immigrant member of the couple to the host culture (Kim et al., 2012; Negy & Snyder, 2007) and positive societal perceptions of intercultural marriage (Reiter & Gee, 2008).

Early research seemed to suggest that not only did intercultural couples struggle with the differences between them, they also suffered from societal discrimination and racism. This may have had—and in some countries may still have—some basis in political reality, for until 1967, for instance, marrying somebody from a different racial group was seen as miscegenation and outlawed in 16 states in the United States. Interracial sexual relationships were, of course, illegal in Nazi Germany, and during apartheid in South Africa. In some countries, it is still especially difficult for couples to marry across religious divides. For example, no religious intermarriages can be performed legally in Israel. In India, the Special Marriage Act was instituted in 1954 to sanction the possibility of marrying across religion. However, intercaste and interreligious marriages are still taboo areas, as evidenced by the recent high rate of honor killings among South Asian communities (United Nations Population Fund, 2000).

In a discursive analysis, Killian (2001a) focused on dominant and marginalized discourses used by interracial couples in the US. At the time, monocultural couples were still seen as the norm by wider society, with discourses of homogamy and color blindness prevailing. Killian found that White partners perceived Black partners' reactions to society's racism as being *hypersensitive*. He used the expression "crossing borders" (Killian, 2001b, 2013) to describe interracial couples in the US visiting all-White or all-Black segregated neighborhoods and to symbolize interracial partners' divergent social locations. Some couples, fearing consequences from being seen as a couple, would utilize strategies such as disassociating from one another and restricting their itineraries (Killian, 2003).

Several authors argue that intercultural couples are more likely to fail (Berman, 1968; Gurung & Duong, 1999; Osanami Törngren, Irastorza, & Song, 2016; Okitikpi, 2009), and experience conflict and unhappiness (Bhugra & De Silva, 2000) than their monocultural counterparts, echoing early sociological and anthropological explanations for the alleged preference for endogamy in societies (Davis, 1941). However, recent studies have challenged this view (Bhugun, 2017; Irastorza & DeVoretz, 2009; Kenney & Kenney, 2012).

Countering this discourse is a body of literature in the USA which has shown that intercultural couples (primarily conceived as "African-Americans" and "European-Americans") may have an increased commitment to each other precisely because of the discrimination they experience in society (Hibbler & Shinew, 2017; Rosenblatt et al., 1995). There is also a strand of quantitative research on "marital satisfaction," showing that intercultural couples are no less satisfied with their marriages than their monocultural counterparts (Gaines & Brennan, 2001). Marital satisfaction is measured using the 15-item ENRICH (Evaluating and Nurturing Relationship Issues, Communication, Happiness) inventory, which is empirically-based (Fowers & Olson, 1993), as well as other measures: Marital Satisfaction Scale (Roach, Frazier, & Bowden, 1981), Marital Satisfaction Inventory (Snyder, 1979), Dyadic Adjustment Scale (Spanier, 1976), and Quality Marriage Index (Norton, 1983). However, intercultural marriage satisfaction is largely under-researched in contrast to monocultural marriages (Forry et al., 2007; Herr, 2009).

Although it may be true that intercultural couples face many challenges and are subject to negative assumptions from society, they also experience benefits. Falicov (1995) identified several opportunities and positive impacts of cultural differences on intercultural couples, such as mutual adaptation and accommodation that can lead to increased cultural sensitivity, understanding and tolerance of diversity, personal transformation, and mutual acculturation. In fact, recent studies (Bhugun, 2017; Caballero et al., 2008; Crippen, 2008, 2011; Heller & Wood, 2000; Killian, 2013; Singla, 2015; Tseng, 2016) have identified new strengths-based factors that have an impact on the experiences of intercultural couples, including that the blending of cultures can enrich interactions and the inclusion of both cultures in the relationship can help partners move beyond seeing cultural differences as a bone of contention.

SIGNIFICANT THEMES AND PROCESSES

Through the review of literature we see recurring interrelated themes emerge, which we also see reflected in our clinical practice. These themes have to do with the meaning of home, power, and gender, language and communication styles, and constructions of love and intimacy. As the Exeter Model originated in treating the presenting problem of depression, we pay particular attention in the IEM model also to how depression may be conceptualized and expressed differently in different cultures. The use of the culturegram, in particular, and the cultural genogram, as well, are particular interventions in the IEM that address them.

Conflict around these themes may be seen as part of, the main, or even inadvertently and unwittingly contributory to, the presenting problem in the IEM. What we often treat and what we can help elucidate, using the interventions outlined in Part 2 of this book, is the conflictual part of being intercultural in the relationship. But we also can bring out the richness of their cultural difference for them.

The Meaning of Home

Conflicts about home and whose territory the couple are living in may occur at different points in the family life cycle. Such conflict may erupt later on in their couple relationship, especially when they have children together and must make decisions about the best country in which to raise their children or whose values/traditions to privilege as they rear their families. The decision about whose territory in which to live may also become salient when parents are aging or when retirement beckons.

When one or both partners in an intercultural couple are migrants, the loss of their home or country of origin may be associated with sadness or grief. Papadopoulos (2002) aptly describes the sense of "nostalgic disorientation" faced by refugees and forced migrants when they have to leave their homes and move to another country. They miss the sights, sounds, tastes, and smells of home, without being consciously aware of what they are missing. Similarly, Falicov (2014) used the idea of ambiguous loss to depict this feeling of disorientation and confusion. These feelings may be compounded by difficulties settling in the host country, problems with visas, and experiences of racism. Political events like Brexit (i.e., the UK planning to exit the European Union) and the instituting of recent immigration policies in the U.S. can have a profound impact on an intercultural couple's sense of safety and belonging in the home country. In other cases, the migrant partner(s) may instead embrace the new country as well as the notion of multiple homes. Hence, the clinician working with intercultural couples should put aside their own assumptions and start with an exploration of the unique significance and meaning of home to each partner in an intercultural couple.

Power and Gender

As addressed in the previous section, one way in which power differences between partners in intercultural couples may be played out is through the choice of where to live. Bhugun (2017) coined the term "righteousness of privilege" to describe another aspect of the power differences between intercultural parents. Bhugun (2017) found that the issue of power may not be evident or acknowledged until it is brought up, usually by the migrant partner. Partners or parents from the host culture may assume that they have the privilege of truth regarding parenting practices. Some migrant partners described feeling powerless from being treated as outsiders regarding their parenting practices (Bhugun, 2017). For example, most of the time, immigrant partners report that in their culture and country, newborn children sleep with the parents in the same bed but are disappointed when their host partners insist that the children should sleep in separate rooms. The immigrant partners may feel powerless because the sleeping pattern of the host culture is imposed on them. An example from the clinical practice of an Australian associate was an Australian host parent who claimed to be "always right" because of the dominant cultural belief that children should not sleep with their parents, and that they should be left to "sleep-cry" despite the partner's different cultural belief that this was inhumane and an "un" familial thing to do. In this example, parenting practices from the host culture are accorded the status of "truths."

Killian (2015) found that problems can arise when partners explicitly or implicitly value their culture of origin over that of their partners. Frequently, the partner with greater accompanying power and privilege (e.g., Western country of origin, lighter skin, upper to upper-middle class, or some intersection of these) presumes that the majority of his or her cultural customs, traditions, and values should become the template for the couple system, and, if children are created, for the new family system. The more privileged partner can view his or her culture's way of seeing the world, managing conflicts, and raising the next generation as "best" or beyond reproach, expecting the other partner to make a case for why his or her values, traditions, and rituals should be included in the first-world order. Alternatively, partners may "sacrifice" their families' histories, identities, and traditions in order to "get along" in the present.

Different cultures may also have vastly different ideas about gendered roles and expectations, and partners who are migrant men or those from minority ethnic groups may be positioned as sexist or dominating. Similarly, women from the host culture may be seen as dominating, opinionated, or "bossy."

However, gender and power are not one-way dimensional processes in intercultural relationships. Some migrant male partners may also lose power when it comes to gender roles in the intercultural family. Although men and women have defined roles in certain ethnic cultures, the inference usually in many cultures is that men are still regarded as the authority in the family and ultimate decision-makers in family processes. This view of power status could be compromised as a result of marrying into a Euro-American culture, which promotes and values equal gender power and rights. For example, most migrant male partners from ethnic cultures do not cook, wash, and put women's clothes on the clothesline. But in many Western cultures, they have started to cook, wash, and hang clothes out to sustain a healthy relationship and family, as well as an adaptive process in the host society. It appears that the shift in power dynamics is also related to the fact that most women work in either full-time or part-time jobs and therefore their husbands have to share the family and parenting responsibilities. Further, the lack of parenting support from extended family members in many Western cultures, as opposed to the support in ethnic families back home, forces men to share in family and parental roles. Interestingly though, the partners from the migrant ethnic cultures revert to their defined roles when they go back to their countries of origin (Singh, Killian, Bhugun, & Tseng, 2020).

Language and Communication Styles

In her seminal research Burck (2005) highlighted the possibilities that speaking a foreign language can create—for example, the ability to experience an emotion like anger in a foreign language, but not in one's native tongue.

Distancing oneself from one's mother tongue can thus be a liberating experience for some migrants. Among intercultural couples, language differences can be used to mark inclusion, exclusion, and power differences. Just as language differences can create dilemmas for intercultural couples, differences in communication styles can also create barriers in intercultural relationships. Communication styles have been found to be different in different cultures, with Western cultures privileging direct, and often assertive, styles of communication and Eastern cultures relying more on indirect communication (Bhugun, 2017; Falicov, 1995; Tamura & Lau, 1992). Clinical work with intercultural couples can help them to recognize the different communication styles that they employ. Further, nonverbal and representational therapeutic techniques such as cultural genograms, ecomaps, and culture-grams may be of great value in bridging verbal impasses that intercultural couples can find themselves in. In the second part of this book, we will explore how we employ two nonverbal techniques—the cultural genogram and the culturegram, in our work with intercultural couples.

Constructions of Love, Intimacy, and Couplehood

In clinical work with a marriage between a Bangladeshi woman born and brought up in the U.K. and her spouse who was born and brought up in Bangladesh that RS conducted, differences about the meaning of romantic love prevailed. The wife, who was far more westernized than her husband, struggled to communicate her romantic feelings, needs for intimacy, and desires to her Bengali speaking husband. "How do I find Bengali words in which to say, 'I love you'?" she asked in therapy.

In many cultures and religions, arranged marriages are the norm and pre-marital sex is prohibited. In such instances and cultural traditions, marrying outside one's own community, religion, and culture can be associated with a sense of loss, dishonor, and betrayal, and may have an impact on the sexual and intimate relationship of a couple who have "transgressed" in these ways. Further, such a couple may come to their relationship with completely different templates of love, intimacy, and togetherness, originating from their different cultural backgrounds. Partners from migrant or minority ethnic backgrounds in which individuals are deeply embedded within extended family relationships—in which the couple is not the primary dyad (Gabb & Singh, 2015b)—may not be able to understand the more first-world construction of the couple as, in those cultures, the primary dyad within the family. In many non-Western cultures, in fact, the primary "dyad" might comprise the father–son, mother–daughter, or other dyads sometimes indeed based on social rather than biological ties. To operate within such cultural configurations to rely solely on the couple relationship for emotional needs and support could result in feelings of loneliness and isolation.

Having a community of other intercultural or mixed couples can help in overcoming the feelings of being alienated by providing a sense of connectedness (Singh, 2014).

The Meaning and Expression of Depression

Symptoms of depression could be linked to any of the themes delineated thus far. Depression, mourning, and bereavement could be associated with the loss of homeland and associated family ties—particularly when there is an illness or death of an elderly parent who lives in another country. Depression could also be associated with cut-offs and losses of religion, culture, and language.

Beyond this, the understanding and interpretation given to "depression" in some cultures, looks, and is understood very differently: depression is thought of as something that is somatized and expressed through bodily symptoms, such as a "sinking heart" (Krause, 1989; Malik, 2000). As clinicians working with intercultural couples, we have to be able to identify and work with different expressions of, understandings of, and interpretations given to, depression, in understanding the different cultural meanings it may have.

The Family Life Cycle

An overarching systemic perspective that has particular relevance to intercultural couples is that of the family life cycle. Systemic theory posits that transitional periods in the family life cycle are vulnerable times for difficulties to erupt; symptoms, therefore, may arise in the transitions between one developmental stage and another. They can signal the family's difficulties in making these transitions (McGoldrick, Garcia Preto, & Carter, 2015). With intercultural couples, an added level of conflict can emerge because of a lack of agreement about the meaning of the religious and cultural practices and the impact of such practices within some of these transition periods; particularly those that center around beliefs and practices of parenting. An example of this is the religious rituals of children's passage from or into adolescence. In Judaism the transition into "adulthood"—or, actually, adolescence toward adulthood, at the age of 13—is marked by the Bar or Bat Mitzvah. In Catholicism an important childhood transition is the First Communion, in which the child is deemed old enough to understand the significance of such an act of worship. When one partner is Jewish and the other Catholic this can bring into focus deeply held beliefs about how and when to mark a child's capacities, and how and when to involve family in doing so. When working with intercultural couples, systemic practitioners can design innovative rituals that incorporate elements of both partners' cultural traditions, in order to facilitate transitions from one developmental stage to another (Singh, 2017).

To conclude, in this chapter we have highlighted a few of the key themes and processes for intercultural couples. We are interested in how the interventions that we describe in the next part of this book are influenced by these themes—for example, how does missing home for a migrant partner in an intercultural couple impact on the presenting problem of depression, and how is this maintained by the communication cycle explicated in our model? How would we intervene, drawing on any of the interventions in the Intercultural Exeter model?

PART 2

The Interventions

INTRODUCTION TO PART 2

In Part 2 of the book we define and describe *each of the interventions* in the IEM, using two clinical cases of couples working with a therapist using the model. For each of the interventions we use the definitions that the Expert Reference Group gave for the agreed-upon best practice interventions, but with a difference: because of the lack of attention to the influence of culture, the IEM interventions all stress that they are done within questioning or explaining that open up the opportunities for the couple to think about things within the frame of their respective cultures. So each of the interventions, as they are defined, have the added instruction, or definition, that they be done to guide such questioning and heighten the couple's cultural consciousness.

We describe the two couples and the reasons they came into therapy and we will show, in a scripted format, how each intervention is employed.

Fiona and Raja

Fiona and Raja are two young professionals, married for 4 years, together for 6.

Fiona, aged 32, comes from a white, British working-class family, with two younger siblings. Her parents were born in Britain and their families have apparently been British for generations.

The genogram (see Chapter 9, in which the definition and illustration of "genogram" appears) shows that Fiona's family was working class: her mother held down a series of clerking positions, but often stopped work because of her bouts of depression, while her father worked at a steel works and was active in his union. When Fiona was in her early teens her father left the family for another woman and began a new family, with whom Fiona has

The Intercultural Exeter Couples Model: Making Connections for a Divided World Through Systemic-Behavioral Therapy, First Edition. Janet Reibstein and Reenee Singh.
© 2021 John Wiley & Sons Ltd. Published 2021 by John Wiley & Sons Ltd.

had little contact. Fiona had an aunt, her mother's sister, who lived not far, with whom she was close. Fiona was closer to her father, and to her aunt, than to her mother, with whom she has had a distant and cold relationship. She felt her mother favored her sister, with whom she did not get along. Her family identified as C of E, but were not religious and Fiona does not see herself as having a religious affiliation.

Fiona attended college and then worked, attending university as a "mature student." She is the first, and, so far, the only one in her family to go on to university, having been academically successful in school, and ambitious for a career and to "make something of herself." She has worked in the tech industry since graduating, and met Raja through mutual friends. They married 2 years later, when Fiona was 28. She had been, since graduation, continually employed, and in a job in which she felt she had flourished, until the couple moved to facilitate Raja's career. She has been out of work since, a situation prolonged because of her depression.

She had a depressive episode at university, with some counseling, but her first clinical depression, in which she was psychiatrically treated with anti-depressants, and at first individual psychodynamic and then couples therapy, occurred after the couple had moved to a new city, which necessitated Fiona leaving her highly prized job, as well as a close set of friends from university and work.

She is not particularly close to her family, although she feels loyal to them and many of their traditions, if not their ideals, which do not include "achievement" nor valuing other cultural traditions, which she says she does.

Raja, 33, is from an upper-middle-class family in which his parents are both highly educated medical professionals. He works in a middle-management job in the pharmaceuticals industry and was recently promoted, which is what prompted their move to a different part of the country. His parents were both medically trained in India. They are first-generation migrants to the UK, having completed their medical trainings there. His mother worked part-time as a GP while Raja was growing up, while his father was a hospital doctor. Their own parents are well-to-do and live very comfortably in India, but have spent long periods in the UK over Raja's life, as he has, in turn, made many visits to his family in India. They are a very close-knit family. He has an older brother who is also a doctor. Raja was the "rebel," getting involved in the music scene at school and university and, instead of doing medicine or science, he decided on a business degree. His job promotion, necessitating the couple's move, was a major precipitant to Fiona's depressive episode.

His parents are practicing Muslims. Although Raja does not see his religion as a defining part of him, he feels respectful toward his parents' practice and belief.

As with many intercultural couples we did a cultural genogram and a culturegram with our two couples first, before we embarked on the central

IEM intervention, the IEM Circularity. These two pictorial interventions are typically accessible ways to get to know clients. But more to the point of our method, they discreetly put the issue of culture front and center, making clients and therapist literally see it from the outset. It is often the case that the cultural differences are obscured, sometimes willfully, perhaps more often unwittingly, as the dominant rhetoric within domestic life in intercultural partnerings is usually one of the "melting pot" of the dominant culture ("what drew us together was how much we had in common across the differences"). By doing these interventions first the meta-message is that culture is a frame through which their lives together should be viewed; the work they will do with you will proceed through this frame, encouraging them to bring in questions and openness to how culture is influencing their lives together and might be creatively and productively utilized.

Helen and Rebecca

Rebecca is 34 and doing her MSc in Cultural Studies, having worked in publishing when she came to the UK after university in Israel, where she grew up. She comes from a very close-knit, exuberant middle-class family, in which her grandparents were Holocaust survivors and her parents academics, her mother is also a practicing doctor. They are politically active, left-wing, and fully supportive of the fact that Rebecca is lesbian. She grew up in an urban, intellectual climate in which some of her parents' close friends and colleagues were, themselves, in same-sex relationships. She is Jewish by culture, although claims to be non-observant, but is very loyal to what she characterizes as Jewish cultural ideas and practices that are not religious, such as being "expressive" and "liberal." She is the middle, and only, daughter of four children. She was formerly in a long-term relationship with another Israeli woman and lived with her for 2 years before meeting Helen. She and Helen have been together for 4 years and have lived together for 2.

Helen is 35, and a deputy head at a secondary school. She is Caucasian, English, although her maternal grandparents were Scottish, with Anglo-Saxon roots as far back as she can track them. She is the only girl, with two brothers, both married with children. Her parents are middle-class: her father owns a small business and her mother has not worked but trained as a nurse. She was closest to her father in her family. She is a non-practicing Catholic, although her mother had been brought up Presbyterian. Helen was brought up Catholic, but has disavowed her faith since university. She was formerly in a heterosexual relationship, when at university, but broke that off when she fell in love with a woman when she moved to London for her first job. At that point she identified as lesbian. She is now not close to her family, who live in the north of England, and who, she says, do not accept or understand her sexuality. For this reason she keeps a distant relationship with them.

The Systemic–Behavioral Interventions

CHAPTER 5

Circularities

Breaking Patterns and Setting the Scene for Establishing New Ones

THE IEM CIRCULARITY INTERVENTION; INTERRUPTING CIRCULARITIES; FINDING POSITIVES

The IEM Circularity Explained

As we described in Chapter 2, the IEM feedback loop—or the "circularities" intervention—is based on couples breaking down, moment-to-moment, within an episode they nominate as typical, and describing, first, the behaviors they make in response to each other, and then the thoughts and feelings that lie behind each of those responses. (The procedure is detailed for you, below.) In so doing they have an opportunity to discover that perhaps they have made inaccurate conclusions and attributions about their partners; that they are learning more, and more clearly getting information about, their partners and giving out the same; and opening up avenues to explore more about themselves and their partners, both in terms of the reasons for their thoughts, feelings, and behaviors, and also in terms of developing new and more adaptive repertoires of behaviors together. Making thoughts and feelings clear and explicit—when they are all too often implicit and assumed— can be key to finding new ways to act and also to understand.

The use of culturally based enquiry fits directly into the use of the circularities intervention. Charting a circularity is meant to lay bare the groundwork for intercultural questions around the "why" around feelings and thoughts—these are often unwittingly governed by family and cultural

The Intercultural Exeter Couples Model: Making Connections for a Divided World Through Systemic-Behavioral Therapy, First Edition. Janet Reibstein and Reenee Singh.
© 2021 John Wiley & Sons Ltd. Published 2021 by John Wiley & Sons Ltd.

practices and beliefs—as well as behaviors—for people do what they, often again unwittingly, expect—and that is grounded in culture. In the example of Raja and Fiona, below, this is what occurs.

The IEM Circularity

In understanding the IEM circularity, first remember that it takes a systemic feedback loop, which connects broad descriptions of who does what in response to the other person around in a circle to see how behavior (productive or non-productive) is mutually maintained. But in a traditional systemic feedback loop, or circularity, thoughts, feelings, and behaviors are all conjoined. The unobserved aspects of people's interactions do not get investigated or disentangled from the observed. The IEM circularity takes a leaf from CBT's book. But CBT's feedback loop is of an *individual's* thoughts, feelings, and behaviors reinforcing each other. It leaves out in this the reinforcing power of the *other person* within *an interaction*.

People develop habits or patterns of behavior together that reinforce each person's thoughts, feelings, and behaviors in relation to the other person. The IEM circularities intervention focuses upon deconstructing this to the level of how this reinforces not just the pattern of observed behavior but the pattern of thoughts and feelings (and thereby maintaining not just the behaviors that might be supporting unproductive patterns, but also the thoughts and feelings, often made up on misconstruals and misconceptions, which themselves maintain the behaviors).

The couple describes the circular pattern. They do so with the purpose of laying it bare for further interrogation. The IEM circularity is the fundament of IEM therapy. It lays the groundwork. It is where the other interventions come into service: the use of the family script intervention, or the cultural genogram, the genogram, or the culturegram, for instance. Or, for some of the other behavioral interventions: trying out "I statements" or "negotiations" instead of the old behaviors laid bare in the circularities investigation.

How Do You Chart an IEM Circularity?

The procedure for charting a circularity is as follows:

- Choose, with the couple, a characteristic episode in which you chart each *behavioral* sequence between the couple.

- This is for showing, first, how the one's behavior (the observable or audible behavior, itself, only) brings a reaction from the other (this can include silence or apparent non-reaction: it is what is observed or heard by the other that is important).

- You then proceed to what reaction on the first person this second person's observed behavior has upon the first.

- And so on you go, in sequence, until at the top of the cycle you see how the presenting symptom (e.g., depression, or arguing, or estrangement, or lack of sex) which was already there at the beginning of the cycle, is being—often unwittingly—maintained by the couple's *behavioral* interactional cycle.[1]

- Then, go back into this cycle, again, once you have finished the *behavioral* sequence, and add in each member of the couple's *thoughts* and *feelings* at each point in the sequence of the cycle.

When you do this cycle with your couple you may have to prompt them around labelling their feelings and occasionally also their thoughts. You may, for instance, use systemic hypothesizing such as "if it were me, I might be feeling x…" which is a way of using the intervention of "normalizing" which we will expand upon in a moment. Or you might use some "circular questioning" (see the description of this intervention in Chapter 8) interventions, such as "If someone outside might be observing this he or she might think you'd be feeling (or thinking) y…" to coach toward what words could describe thoughts and feelings. When you introduce words to describe what feelings might typically arise in a given situation under investigation, you are teaching what is expectable—this is the intervention called "normalizing." Part of the function of "normalizing" can be that it can act as psychoeducation (see description in Chapter 8). For people can struggle to describe or label feelings and often confuse thoughts and feelings with each other.

This illustrates one way in which the circularity intervention forms a substrate from which to access and use other interventions.

(To review the circularities in action, go to Chapter 3, and also see, below, a snapshot from their therapy.)

EXAMPLE

Fiona and Raja

Fiona: I just feel like a worthless child and that Raja is the one who does everything so much better than me. So sometimes I can't get out of bed I feel so bad. And then Raja sees that and withdraws and goes upstairs. It's like he just can see what's going to happen next and sort of checks out and that leaves me feeling worse. So I want to escape and be with my mates who make me have fun.

---

[1] i.e., people can often think they are being helpful because either they are motivated by caring and do not want to push or risk causing harm, pain, or sadness—or, more pertinently, they do not know what can or will help or not.

Therapist responds to Fiona: So when you feel hopeless, Fiona, you leave: you go out and see your mates? That is what you *do* when you see Raja doing something—that is, when what you see is that he is withdrawing and going upstairs, right? The point is—just let me be clear—you two haven't talked, you just have seen that he is going upstairs, right? And he just sees what you are doing, too—I mean, you haven't talked—so he sees you leave. Right?

So, Fiona, I am going to put this on the circle: under "B" for your "behavior"—that is the only thing that Raja actually sees, you see. You go. You leave.

Now, under "F" for how you "feel" I am going to write "hopeless." Raja doesn't really see that. He might guess that. But he also might guess something else. This could be the first time he hears clearly what was going on inside you, and maybe he had other ideas about what was, you know? And then under "T" for "thoughts"—and Raja doesn't know what those were, just like feelings because they're inside you till you talk and tell—they are "I am a worthless child and Raja does everything better than me. If I go be with my mates I'll at least have some fun and feel better."

Fiona: Yes.

Therapist: And, Fiona, when we did your genogram and culturegram we saw that your own mother had been depressed and your father was very competent, you said, and your mother used to feel useless. And that she was expected to work, because the women in your family, your culture—unlike Raja's—always had to work to help out, but because of her depression she couldn't hold down jobs so she'd feel more useless. Is that right?

Fiona: Yeah. And now I don't have a job. So I think about that, too.

Therapist: I'm going to add under "T" for thought: "In my culture I think I should have a job to feel worthwhile."

Fiona: nods.

Therapist: And then, Raja: You have just heard more about what went on for Fiona, what was inside her, in her thoughts and feelings and how they might have been formed differently from yours. You didn't know this, before, at least not for sure, I think, because all you really knew is what you saw. Is that right?

Raja: Yeah. I sort of guessed at things, but, yeah, that's all I saw.

Therapist: Okay, so now let's see what happens with you in response to what you saw. You will have made a response, and that's all Fiona will have seen, and you'll have had thoughts and feelings based on what you saw and how that made you think and feel. So let's start with what did you do when you saw that she left?

Raja: I sat in my room and just stared. Then I thought I have to find her. But that was after. Because first I feel rejected and miserable. And I think I have to find her. She needs me. And I worry and then I text her and tell her I'm worried.

Therapist: Okay, so we're going to write that what at first you did was "withdraw"—sit and do nothing, not reaching out to Fiona, at first, and then you text. That's all she sees, by the way. Unless you told her that you sat and withdrew and were miserable she wouldn't for sure know that. We're going to write for "F" you feel rejected, worried, and miserable. And for the "T" "I have to find her. She needs me." So all Fiona really "knows" is from the behavior she sees: the text that says you are worried about her. And Raja, we know from your genogram and culture-gram that in your family and where they come from it is very clearly the duty of the "man of the family" to be strong and to make sure that the women are safe and looked after. By the way, in your heritage it isn't so important for a woman to work, is it? I mean, I think you said that there's a slight sense that it detracts from the man's position if his wife works, like he isn't providing enough or some-thing, is that right? Also, I know from what you both told me that in your family, Fiona, women drank. It was acceptable, even if you and your mother both did it too much even for your family. But in your culture and family women did not drink. It was much less acceptable for a woman to drink alcohol than a man. Is that true?

Raja: Yeah. Especially about the drink. I could never tell my parents that Fiona drinks, at least more than a glass of wine or beer occasionally. And about the work, well, my parents are a bit more modern—my mother had a profession and worked part-time, but they definitely do think the man's job is more important. I don't really believe that, but that was what my grandparents definitely believed and in their country it was true.

Therapist: Okay. So what do you do when you get that text, Fiona?

Fiona: I don't do anything. I feel sick with guilt. Like I can't move. I am being bad to him and for him. So I think I should just stay away from him. It'd be better. And I stay away. Sometimes for a day or more. So I drink more.

Therapist: Okay, so we are going to write what Raja "sees" in response to what he's done: "B" is "does nothing." And "T" is "I am being bad to him and I'm bad for him. It's better if I stay away. I better drink more not to feel so bad." And "F" is "I feel guilty."

Fiona: Yeah.

Therapist: And Raja? You see her "B"—she doesn't respond—what happens for you? What do you do then?

Raja: I get worried and I think she has to know this and she's just being terrible to me if she knows this and so then I get angry. So I text her angry texts.

Therapist: So your "B" in response to her "do nothing"—though you don't at this point know why she's doing nothing; you don't know she feels so guilty and thinks she's bad so it's better for you both if she stays away and all that—so you now, now you get angry. Because you are worried—we'll put that down as "F" along with "angry" and the "T" is because you think she must know you're worried and she's just being cruel to you by not answering then.

Fiona: So then I see those angry texts and they are just what I thought: I am bad for him. He's angry at me. So I feel worse but then I also get scared because he's angry. So I don't answer and think I shouldn't go home as I'll only make it worse then. Why should I go home? I contribute nothing but to making him angry.

Therapist: So you stay away longer? You go silent then?

Fiona: Yes.

Therapist: So again, "B" is "do nothing" in response to Raja. "F" is "scared" also still "guilty" and "worthless"—and "T" is "I shouldn't go home as it will only make it worse as I contribute nothing except to his anger."

Raja: And then I just feel depressed. She clearly doesn't care. So I stop texting.

Therapist: So you only see that she has not responded. You don't know those thoughts and feelings. You conclude from her non-action that she "clearly doesn't care"—that's your "T" here on the circle at this point. Your feelings are "depressed." And I guess "uncared for." Not, I guess, so angry anymore, and not, I see, unlike what Fiona has concluded, that it's better she stays away or that she contributes nothing.

Raja: No, not at all. By the way, I don't care if she doesn't have a job right now, because I know she will get one again. I believe in her. I want her to work but not because I think she's useless without a job. Maybe in my family I don't see the pressure on her from hers. But maybe she thinks I don't care if she works if my family doesn't approve. I only just thought of that now.

Fiona: That's interesting. But look, when he goes silent then I get worried. I think maybe there's something wrong with him. I'd better go home and see. It's like that takes over. So then I decide to come home. I text him and say sorry and that I'm on my way. That's when I stop drinking and come home.

Therapist: So—interesting. In the "B" you respond to him by text to his stopping, or his non-action in response to your non-action. And your "F" is "worried." Not guilty or so worthless so much anymore. At least they recede in response to his silence. And your "T" is "I'd better see if he's okay. And I'd better stop drinking." So what does Raja do when you come through the door?

Raja: I get angry at her at first. I start to shout. But then when I see her, I really am so relieved she's okay, so I put my arms around her—I want her to know I am so glad she is back—and we cry together.

Therapist: So in the "B" I will put "shouts" then "embraces" then "cries," and in "F" I will put "angry" then "relieved" and "glad," and in "T" I'll write "She's okay," and "I am glad she is back and want her to know."

Therapist: And Fiona, then? What happens then?

Fiona: I say I'll stop drinking. I am glad I am home. I am happy to be with Raja. But I still feel guilty. Very guilty. And he's like the grown-up and I was the naughty child who just came home from running away. So I feel glad to be with him but worthless and like a child. I just showed I need him to take care of me.

Therapist: Okay. So in "B" you tell him you won't drink. In "T" you think "I am still a child and I need him to take care of me." And "I just showed that I need him to take care of me." And in "F" you feel "glad" but also, and it sounds mostly, "guilty" and "worthless." So, we are looking at how the typical interactions between the two of you might be unwittingly keeping you depressed. Up here, at the top of the circle, of this cycle of interactions of your thoughts, feelings, and behaviors are you still depressed?

Fiona: Yes.

Therapist: So you have just shown how you are helping each other without knowing it to keep the depression going. What is interesting is how much each of you is only reacting at every point to what you think the other one must be thinking and feeling but you don't know. And if you did, you might be able to do different things in response to each other. And maybe change the way you both feel.

So let's go back over this cycle. Fiona, it sounds as if, for instance, you think Raja is feeling fed up with you or something when he goes upstairs, and then you conclude that you're worthless to him and should leave to be with people who can make you feel not so worthless. But we can see from this cycle we've charted that that isn't what he's feeling. In fact, he's feeling useless, himself. And his family and cultural expectations that he be the one to "save" you, make him feel even more this way.

Therapist: So what we've done is looked at the ways you both behave—what you two do—in reaction to each other, without really knowing what the other was thinking and feeling. And you didn't really know a lot that was completely accurate, right? So now we've put some of that right, do you think at each point one or both of you could do something different? Not go upstairs, for instance? Not go out of the house? Say something about how you're feeling instead? Not respond to a text? Not go silent? All sorts of other choices at any of these points could mean a different outcome at the end: that is, not maintaining the depression!

Interrupting Circularities: (A Step Toward Changing Them Toward More Adaptive and Productive Ones)

Challenging the repetitive patterns and sequences, for example by:

• Interrupting monologs, or cycles of accusation, rebuttal, and counter-accusation.

• Exploring possible functions performed by such repetitive sequences for each partner and the couple.

• Tracking and reflecting back observations about patterns of relating and their possible purposes for each partner and the couple.

• Replaying and highlighting key interactions so they can be more directly experienced in the session.

• Providing opportunities for each partner to imagine what they think might happen if existing roles and relationship patterns were to change.

• Identify recurring behavior and feelings that might act as flashpoints for each partner in their relationship, explore the contexts in which they arise.

• Doing each of these within a "cultural frame"—that is, wondering if there is a connection to their respective ideas passed down through families and cultures—with reference to their genograms, culturegrams, and scripts—that could be contributing?

EXAMPLE

Fiona and Raja
Therapist: So, Raja, when you see Fiona in bed how can you do something different even if you begin to feel hopeless or useless?
Raja: I don't know. I just feel useless.
Therapist: But Fiona's just been clear to you that you are very useful when she feels bad. She actually would be helped by you doing something that shows she's important to you. Not useless, but useful, it seems!
Raja: I guess I could give her a cuddle or something. Something like that.

Finding Positives

Enabling partners to identify and achieve specific changes they want to make in themselves irrespective of whether their partner reciprocates, including:

- Changes of a broad nature, such as improving the emotional climate of the relationship through being more available to share time.

- Changes with a specific focus, such as the manner in which concerns are raised.

- Encouraging partners to predict how changes in their own behavior might have a positively reinforcing effect upon their partner:

- Exploring how this prediction looks to the partner.

- Exploring their own and their partner's response to initiating such change.

- Encouraging partners to check out the validity of attributions they make about each other.

- Encouraging partners to check out the validity of perceived (as compared with actual) criticism.

- Doing each of these within a "cultural frame"—that is, wondering if there is a connection to their respective ideas passed down through families and cultures—with reference to their genograms, culturegrams, and scripts—that could be contributing?

EXAMPLE

Fiona and Raja
Therapist to Fiona: So if things were different between you, if Raja were to come over to you and talk, rather than go upstairs and withdraw when he thinks you are depressed, how would that be?
Fiona: I would feel supported.

Therapist: Has Raja ever done that?

Fiona: Sure. He can do that. He does sometimes. But I think that in his culture men don't so much talk about feelings and that is probably why I also feel guilty for having feelings that need to be talked about! When he sees me lying in bed he thinks it's worse than ever and he gives up.

Therapist: But if he did come over and talk you'd find that helpful? Maybe because in your culture you can give words to how to talk about feelings you could give some pointers for Raja. Maybe he'd find it helpful to know what you think would help to say or ask?

Fiona: Yes, he could say, "Hey, I see you might not be feeling okay. But let's do something together when I get home tonight." Just that would make me feel better. Nothing big. Not a big talk. Just something. Make me feel he wants me.

CHAPTER 6

Communication Training

ACTIVE LISTENING

This is an exercise to help people change their habits of not listening well on the one hand and not waiting to ensure they have been properly heard and understood on the other. It is meant to help people realize how they are missing the meanings and shared understandings from each other because they are not either listening well, with the intention of trying to understand fully what the other is saying, and also by rushing to say things without ensuring that what you are saying has been properly stated and received. It entails:

- Encouraging partners to listen actively (clarifying but not debating what is being said) in a manner that supports and validates the speaker.
- Encouraging partners to summarize and reflect back what they have heard, especially in relation to key issues voiced.
- Discouraging either partner from making unfounded assumptions about communications.
- Procedure:
  - One person speaks—only up to a few sentences (the therapist tells the ground rules first, and then halts the speaker if it is going on too long; people can only take in information in small bites).
  - The listener just listens without interrupting and then is asked to say back what the listener thinks the speaker has said.
  - The speaker checks out that the listener has understood what the speaker has said and adds or corrects if there is something to be added or corrected.

The Intercultural Exeter Couples Model: Making Connections for a Divided World Through Systemic-Behavioral Therapy, First Edition. Janet Reibstein and Reenee Singh.
© 2021 John Wiley & Sons Ltd. Published 2021 by John Wiley & Sons Ltd.

- The listener says back then what he/she now does understand the speaker has said.

- The speaker checks out that it is completely understood to his/her satisfaction.

- This operation is then repeated with the speaker/listener roles reversed.

- This is often a most useful exercise when the couple are clearly not hearing, understanding, or listening and the therapist can halt things and ask them to do this exercise on a small piece of what should be heard and understood.

EXAMPLE

Raja and Fiona
Fiona: When I can't get up in the morning—like when you and I haven't been getting along and I feel useless—I just want you to understand how hard it is for me. Especially when you just bound out of bed and just don't even seem to notice....
Therapist: Okay. Thanks, Fiona. Now, Raja, you are going to say back to Fiona just what you heard. Not what you are wanting to say back or anything. Just that you have really heard her.
Raja: Okay. So I heard you say that you sometimes can't get up in the morning after we haven't been getting along, and that you at those times wake up feeling "useless"—and it's hard for you to see me just getting up and "bounding up"—and you want me to understand how hard it is for you then, that you're feeling like that. And, I guess, that it's hard if you think I'm just not noticing....
Therapist (to Fiona): Did he get it? Get it all?
Fiona: Yes. Yes, that's it.

CLEAR AND DIRECT SIMPLE STATEMENTS

This is to help train people to ensure that what they are saying is able to be processed—that it is not too long nor complex for someone to "get" what's being said—and to ensure that they are being clear about what they wish to say.

- Encouraging concise, specific, and relevant speech.

- Use explanatory techniques to aid communication by clarifying what has been said.

- Providing feedback about a communication.

- Reconstructing the content of a message, especially where contradictions may be embedded within it.

- Encouraging direct rather than ambiguous statements.

EXAMPLE

Rebecca and Helen

Rebecca: You are always upsetting me, Helen. Everything you do, it just drives me crazy! Everything!!

Helen: What am I supposed to do with that? Everything? Everything about me you just can't accept?

Therapist: We talked about different styles and different cultural heritages in the past, and I am wondering if in Rebecca's culture and family exaggerating might be happening to make a really strong emotional point? So we might be keeping that in mind, for that is so different from yours, Helen. But we might also think about how it could be helpful for Helen to understand, yes, that for you, Rebecca, things she does sometimes really, really upset you, but which are the specific things?

Rebecca: Yes—it's that it really upsets me, but, of course, not every single thing about Helen. About you, Helen! But, okay, here's one thing that really does drive me crazy: when I am not even yet conscious, first thing in the morning, I'm still in bed and she's already nagging me about something I'm supposed to be doing or haven't yet done. I mean, really!

Therapist: So you get upset when you experience Helen "nagging" you. And it's particularly hard for you when you're just getting up, not yet, as you said, "conscious" even?

Rebecca: Yes. That's it.

Therapist: So maybe Helen you might want to be clear about what Rebecca thinks of as nagging?

Helen: Yeah. I mean I don't think just asking simple questions is "nagging."

Rebecca: I mean when you ask me to do something that I clearly can't yet be doing—I'm only just waking up—so of course it feels like nagging. I can't be doing it then, can I?

Therapist: Thank you, Rebecca, for clarifying. Helen?

ENCOURAGING POSITIVES

This is to train people to express positives; it is much more likely for something to be heard and taken in if it is expressed within a frame of positivity and appreciation; communication flows and is most effective when people know that it is being held within a context of appreciation.

- Encouraging the expression of appreciation, especially before raising concerns.

- Using silence while actively and supportively listening.

- Helping couples define problems in ways that can limit complaint or criticism, for example by encouraging partners to convey why the problem is important to them.

- Using specific examples when raising potentially contentious issues

- Including clear statements about how the problem makes them feel.

EXAMPLE

Helen and Rebecca

Therapist: So it might be helpful for Rebecca to hear what you think, Helen, she *is* getting right for you; sometimes if people only hear what they're getting wrong they really can't see what they're getting right for each other! Let's see what's going right, and then we can explore both how to do more of that and also what she could be doing differently....

Helen: Well, okay. But it's hard when she's always so resentful if I spend time with my parents. I know that she thinks they don't like her. It's not that. They don't approve of what they call our "lifestyle" but they are trying. And they haven't really met any Jews before in their life. They just need to get used to her, and her different style. But that's not the only thing—it's that her parents don't really like me, either, and she doesn't support me enough about that. I mean they want me to be all over them, all sort of loud and tell them everything—that's what they do, I mean, they're Israeli, aren't they?

Therapist: Helen, I can see it's hard. When we're distressed about things it's really hard to shift our focus and we think it's all, it's only, about the bad stuff. Sometimes that's very useful to do, especially when we're trying to solve problems and our attention needs to be drawn to the problem. But sometimes to solve it we also need to widen our focus, and see what we do that does work. I'm wondering if Rebecca might want to hear what she does that does work for the two of you?

Rebecca: Yeah. It would be good to know I'm good at something!

Helen: Oh, of course you are! One of the best things about Rebecca is that she really, really appreciates my work. She really "gets" what it's like to be a journalist and she really knows how to read and help me think about my work. I know not everyone gets that in their relationship and I'm really lucky to have that with her. It's one of the best things about us, together. We can really talk about work and also about books and people. We can talk. Really well. Only when it comes to family. Then our differences and their differences really get in the way.

Therapist: That's really interesting, and helpful. I'm going to try to help you both think about how that "talking" well and that mutual understanding and appreciation that comes out over work, and books, and people, for instance, might be able to grow, and to help you around that area that you say is the problem: your family and all those differences.

"I" STATEMENTS

This helps people avoid "mind-reading" and attributing motivations that may or may not be accurate; it helps people focus upon their own experiences within interactions and taking responsibility for locating them internally, while inviting the other person to consider their part of the interaction in return.

- Promoting "I" statements (rather than "We" or "You" statements that attribute meanings and intentions to others).

- Making sure that statements are phrased so that the speaker is not "mind-reading" or attributing motives to the other person as an explanation.

- Making sure that statements are phrased so that the speaker is speaking from a position of how it strikes, seems, or feels to them—from their own perceptions and experiences.

- This is to lessen attributions of blame and to open up possibilities of "curiosity" about the other person so the other person can explain themselves.

EXAMPLE

Helen and Rebecca

Rebecca: You make me end up screaming at you: you always want me to be the bad guy!

Therapist: Rebecca, you are telling Helen what she does, as you are experiencing it, but you are also telling her why she does it, and that may not be, in fact, her intention: that is, she may not be trying to make you "the bad guy." You might be right, but you can't be sure, can you, till you ask her. You can be sure of your own experience of her behavior. So if you say that, she'll know how her behavior, in itself, is affecting you. It's your experience.

It helps for us to use words that make that clear: "I feel x," or "My experience of your doing x is y." Can you try to say your experience of this?

Rebecca: Ok. I'll try: Helen, when you ask me to pick up my clothes on the floor when I'm just waking up, not yet out of bed, it makes me feel guilty and frustrated and that I've been a bad girl. And then I scream and feel even more like a bad girl because you don't scream—that's not what your family, your "polite culture," does!

PROVIDING CONTEXT FOR SAFE COMMUNICATION

- Softening the way concerns are introduced and voiced.

- Discouraging ending on a criticism when positive statements are made.

EXAMPLE

Helen and Rebecca

Helen: Rebecca, you really are just a mess! You just cannot keep up anything—you're supposed to be in charge of paying just the minimum of our bills and they are always behind and always you can't find them. I mean, how am I supposed to live with this: your life is just a big mess and it's making mine a mess, too!

Therapist: Helen, underneath your anger, which Rebecca really hears, I think, is something else: I wonder if you are really, really distressed, and worried, about Rebecca's disorder, in particular, over your finances?

Helen: Of course I am! I am panicked! And I am also alarmed because it's very hard to see her like this—a mess! So it's both—worry for me and worry for her.

Therapist: And so it's hard for you to say this, to make room for your distress, maybe because you are afraid that Rebecca just will fall apart more, become more a "mess"?

Helen: Yes, I think that's right. I am afraid. Of her breaking, really.

Therapist: Okay, I get that. But I have to remind you that last time you said you were so pleased that Rebecca had been able to pay her student registration not just on time, but early. And that she had set up a standing order for her to you for the mortgage so you wouldn't argue about that anymore. Am I right in remembering that you felt more secure, had more confidence in Rebecca after that?

Helen: Yes, you're right....

Therapist: That was heartening.

Helen: Yes. Yes, it was.

Therapist: So, I wonder if she also can remember your appreciation for this. And I wonder if you can let her know that her efforts then really heartened you?

Helen: Yeah sure. Rebecca, I know you can do stuff. I saw you do those two things and I was so happy and pleased because it was good for you and also it helped me. It really was good.

STRUCTURING

These are interventions that are helpful in breaking down complex issues so that people can more constructively and competently think about the separate issues, themes and difficulties within them.

They are interventions providing a structured and stepped approach to problem-focused discussions, for example by:

- Separating the process of sharing thoughts and feelings from discussions about the way in which decision-making and problem-solving will proceed.

- Developing communication skills before applying them to problem-solving.

- Starting with low conflict before proceeding to high conflict issues.

- Addressing one problem at a time.

- Avoiding being side tracked.

- Discouraging disagreements when there is insufficient time to address them.

- Using open-ended questioning.

- Extending the issue being discussed.

EXAMPLE

Helen and Rebecca

Helen: I don't know where to start. When Rebecca gets into this stressed state, and she gets hysterical, and everything just falls apart. I mean, how are we supposed to get anything done? I mean I sometimes work at home and I need to know that I am not going to be snowed under by all of her stress and chaos. And how am I supposed to be able to be attracted to someone who just can't seem to keep anything together? And who is supposed to be finishing her Masters soon so she can go back to work? I mean we can't afford for her to not work. We really can't.

Therapist: Okay. So, there's quite a lot there. So let's try to slow this process down.... We don't have too much time left today. So can we agree that we will begin to take up just one part of this—perhaps what to do if and when you have to work at home during this period—and contract to continue this, to make sure we "nail it" for you both, in our appointment next week, and then take up the other points: we can make sure we take them up, and put in time for each, in turn.

PROBLEM-SOLVING—HELPING COUPLES FIND A SOLUTION TO IDENTIFIED SPECIFIC PROBLEMS

These are interventions designed to break specific problems down into manageable pieces to get to solutions more constructively and competently. They entail:

- Defining problems.

- Brainstorming potential positive alternatives to current problematic behavior.

- Evaluating the pros and cons of those alternatives.

- Negotiating alternatives.

- Identifying the components of a contract.

- Forming an explicit (when appropriate, written) contract.

- Being able to differentiate between soluble and insoluble problems, and where problems are insoluble maintaining a dialog round the insoluble problem.

- Doing each of these within a "cultural frame"—that is, wondering if there is anything that might be coming through from their respective cultures in the form of ideas or expectations passed down through families and cultures—with reference to their genograms, culturegrams, and scripts— that should be thought through as part of the problem-solving.

EXAMPLE

Raja and Fiona

Fiona: Well, Raja's family is coming over to celebrate my getting this new job. This wasn't my idea, but I know it's important for Raja to show his family that I do work, I am "worth" something. But here's the thing: If I'm celebrating then I want to be able to have a drink. And Raja is saying that he absolutely does not want me to have even one tiny drink in front of his parents. So it's not going to feel at all like it's a celebration for me. It's going to feel like I'm performing again, for them.

Raja: That isn't it at all. I want her to be happy with my family. I want my family to be happy with her. My mum has been hounding me with all sorts of questions about Fiona's new job. She's really excited for her. So I want this to be a great occasion and I don't know what having a drink has to do with that? I mean, is she really so drink dependent that she just has to have one? My family she knows is against drink especially for a woman.

Therapist: Okay. Thanks for laying it out for me, and I'm just going to put stuff on the board for us to help think our way through this one. (writes on the board): "Joint celebration for Fiona and family." Drink is a cultural issue.

Are you both saying: "A celebration of something you're all happy about can be something that cements." (writes on board).

Both nod.

Therapist: So, if you both agree on that, we can start: What are some ideas you can throw out to me, just brain storming, about how to "celebrate" with "all together."

Raja: Have a meal together.

Fiona: Have a drink together.

Therapist: Do both of those things have to be with "everyone" for it to be a celebration?

Raja: Why couldn't it just be a meal though, this time and a drink to celebrate something else next time?

Therapist: Well, that might be a way you could go. I'll write that down.

Fiona: Or it could be that we just have a drink with just us and a meal with just his family?

Therapist: I'm writing that down, too. What might be the pros and cons of each of those ideas?

Fiona: Well, with the first we might forget to "even" it out the next time: we'd have to be kind of keeping score, wouldn't we? But I can see that it might be kind of neater that way. And I don't really "need" the drink, by the way. It's just the way my family always did a special thing: to toast the person with some special drink. And my friends, and what we always did at Uni. You know—just what you do!

Raja: Yeah, but with the second one, would you really feel like it was "celebrating" if we didn't have a drink with the meal, like toasting you in front of my family? Because I can see that the first would be nice and easy—I don't mind keeping track: you know what I'm like. I'm good at that record keeping stuff!

Fiona: No, I think I'd feel okay, because it would be special, like, with you just toasting me. Just toasting me is good: I want that and it could be from just you!

Therapist: Okay. So if you think about those pros and cons, do you think you can at this point make a decision or would you like to think a bit more?

> Because what you're going to do is decide, together, and then do it, and then debrief each other on how it went, and we'll do that here, too, and see if we can "fine-tune" things about encounters with Raja's family, especially over any issues or episodes that could arise like that again, so we can work on other solutions if it didn't work, or make slight adjustments, or whatever.

NEGOTIATION

These are interventions ensuing from "problem-solving," taking them steps further to delineate the parts each person can play within the problem-solving solution process, including each person's personal offers as well as boundaries. They include:

Establishing useful boundaries around emotional expression through:

- Scheduling mutually agreed times and places in which to discuss feelings, especially those associated with painful experiences, whether shared or separate.

- Encouraging partners to accept the importance of other relationships (such as friends and relatives) to provide additional emotional support, and to reduce unmanageable pressure on the relationship, while also:

- Identifying and agreeing upon mutually acceptable boundaries (such as, for example, mutually agreed sexual or financial limits to other relationships).

- Doing each of these within a "cultural frame"—that is, wondering if there is anything that might be coming through from their respective cultures in the form of ideas or expectations passed down through families and cultures—with reference to their genograms, culturegrams and scripts—that should be thought through as part of the negotiating.

EXAMPLE

Fiona and Raja

Fiona: So, we tried to work out a time to do our special celebration, when Raja and I just have our toasting drink. And I realized that I would want it to be really quite special, or it would be meaningless, so I wanted us to go out to dinner and do it, just ourselves, then, and he didn't want to, because he thought that would make a mockery of going out to dinner with his family, like it was second best with them, and so we should just have dinner at home. Like, I mean he said he'd cook. But I know that would mean a takeaway…. Anyway, we started to talk about it, and it was late at night, and we ended up in a fight.

Therapist: Well, good for you both for trying, for really taking this problem-solving seriously. But I suppose it would have helped for us to lay down some tips, or ground rules, whenever you're going to be talking about "hot" subjects. So maybe not late at night?

Raja: Of course, but the problem is that that's kind of the only time we seem to be able to see each other to have any long conversations. I've been traveling for work, Fiona's been doing some courses now, intensive courses in IT, so she can be up to speed once she starts and she's knackered and gets home late, too.

Fiona: Yeah, it's true, but I could definitely come back home on Tuesdays and Thursdays by six. I only stay on to do a little extra work and practice and then I go out with Marie only because I think you're not going to be home till late. So if I come home by six what about you?

Raja: Yeah, sure. I was coming home late because I thought you were, too, so I was grabbing the extra hour or so to catch up at work. But I don't have to. So on those two days, let's in fact go to the Royal Oak and we can talk there, and no one has to worry about cooking. Let's just do that. But I probably would have to get back to do a bit of work maybe for an hour or so.

Fiona: Yeah, that's fine. It'd just be for dinner time. I'm happy to catch up on something on Netflix while you go back to work. As long as it's just an hour?

Therapist: That all sounds a great suggestion, and you both gave something and suggested something and each gave up something as well as offered. And both bounded it, which was good: Tuesday and Thursday nights. After six. At dinner time and at the local.

EMOTIONAL REGULATION IN PROBLEM-SOLVING

These are interventions to help people reach solutions during discussions around problem-solving so that their emotions are kept manageable and understandable during the process.

- Generating an agreed name for problematic repetitive encounters to help them call "time-out."

- Stepping back from their concerns and take a descriptive rather than evaluative stance.

- Describing the sequence of actions they take during problematic encounters to build awareness of the triggers that activate and escalate their feelings.

- Describing the meanings, thoughts, and feelings that accompany escalating arguments.

- Teaching individual self-soothing techniques when possible, inviting and enabling partners to help each other implement self-soothing techniques.

- Encouraging expression of information about feelings as well as reports of thoughts and experiences.

- Tracking the emotions of each partner, as signaled within sessions through verbal and nonverbal cues.

- Doing each of these within a "cultural frame"—that is, wondering if there is a connection to their respective ideas passed down through families and cultures—with reference to their genograms, culturegrams, and scripts— that could be helpful in thinking through around emotions and their expressions.

EXAMPLE

Fiona and Raja

Therapist: So that's all very good, but can we also agree on some further boundaries. I know you've told me about one incident when Fiona, you walked out of a restaurant when you two were having an argument that got too hot. And then things got worse. So, it's a good idea to try to have dinner out, in a neutral space, where often that helps people stay calmer, in public. But sometimes even that doesn't completely work and you need clearer "rules" around talking about "hot" things.

Raja: Well, I know that, in school, teachers used to use "time-out" when kids were getting out of control (laughs).

Fiona: Don't laugh. I think that's a good idea.

Therapist: "Time-out" isn't just for kids. We all do it, inside ourselves, usually uncon- sciously when we know we are being overwhelmed. Sometimes we don't catch it in time, and so we need overt signs: signs for time-out like in sports: The "T" signal of one hand on top of the other, for instance. And then it's time for a break. When we can cool down. Distract ourselves from thinking even for a split second about the distressing thing. Take deep breaths.

Fiona: Or go to the Ladies'. Or Men's.

Raja: As long as we agree, in advance, that that's what that means, and you'll be coming back.

Therapist: Yes, that's part of setting the boundaries: you know what they are and what they mean.

Fiona: Yeah, that's ok. We might have to get up and separate ourselves to calm down and be reasonable with each other. I can signal—that "T sign"—and then get up, and you'd know I was coming back.

Raja: And, obviously, same for me.

CHAPTER 7

Behavioral Action Interventions

ENACTMENTS

Enactments are the use of actions within the sessions that enable partners to try out different approaches to managing conflict, for example by:

- Enacting arguments in the safety of the therapy session.

- Encourage scene setting to provoke the usual emotional affect before then;

- Interrupting enacted arguments to explore alternative approaches.

- Encouraging pretend or controlled arguments outside sessions.

- Using desensitizing techniques to reduce the impact of problematic behavior (such as practicing arguments in sessions).

EXAMPLE

Helen and Rebecca

Therapist: Let's try something. Helen, can you show me what you do when you have found an unpaid bill that you think Rebecca should have paid? And then, Rebecca, show me what you do in response. Let's pretend you're at home, Helen has just come home, and you, Rebecca, have been working at home, it's the end of the day, and Helen has discovered something. Helen, help me out in setting the scene: What kind of thing would happen?

Helen: Well, I normally go in first to the kitchen, and we have a table where the post comes in, and there's usually a pile of papers and stuff on that table, too. Stuff that needs seeing to, or hasn't yet been thrown away. So sometimes I look at that

The Intercultural Exeter Couples Model: Making Connections for a Divided World Through Systemic-Behavioral Therapy, First Edition. Janet Reibstein and Reenee Singh.
© 2021 John Wiley & Sons Ltd. Published 2021 by John Wiley & Sons Ltd.

first thing, after the post, and before I go in to Rebecca's study to say hello. So that's where I might find a bill that she hasn't managed to put away into her study where she'd deal with it. So last week, that bill, that one that had red on it, she hadn't managed to move it, to hide it from me....

Therapist: Okay. So let's pick up from there. You've just found it, and I want you to replay the argument, here, play it out, so I can see how you do this, what happens. You're in Rebecca's study now.

Helen: Okay. Here goes (cool and collected): Rebecca, I cannot believe this! This bill is two months overdue. And it's from your university. You are going to be thrown out. I mean it!! How did this happen? How could you not pay this after all we've gone through, after all we'd agreed on? I mean, do you just not care? Did you not have the money, or what?

Rebecca: (heatedly) Okay. There you go again. Just on your goddamn high horse, up there on the moral high ground. It is no big f-ing deal. Really. You do not have to get all upset about it. I cleared it with the damned university and it's really none of your business. In fact, what in the hell are you doing rooting around in my papers for?

Helen: (in a quiet voice) Rooting around? You are so disorganized you even can't be organized enough to hide this from me!

Rebecca: (starting to screech) That really is it. That really is! Everything comes back to that, doesn't it? Everything is about my failings! My chaos!

She gets up to walk out.

Therapist: Okay. Rebecca, thank you, and can you come back here, sit down, and we can begin to calm down. (Takes a moment while Rebecca does). That was so helpful for me to see how you "do" your arguments, each of you. So thank you, Helen, and I hope you are taking this time to calm yourself, too. You will both be distressed, in your own ways, one showing it more, but the other also distressed. This is good that you are now also showing you can calm yourselves after distress.

So, now, you both seem in a more calm state. Yes?

They nod.

Therapist: So, now, we can try taking it a step further, and differently: let's carry on *discussing* this issue. Rebecca, can you turn to Helen and tell her how you feel when Helen comes in to you having found an unpaid bill?

Rebecca: Well, I feel ashamed. I should have paid. But I did, this time, make arrangements to pay it in installments. And I put a note in my calendar about when the next bill is coming in so I will be prepared. I am learning. But I feel like she doesn't give me the benefit of the doubt, and I feel ashamed.

Therapist: Helen, I know you have told me that you feel impatient when Rebecca tells you she is changing, but how do you feel about hearing her now?

Helen: I don't feel impatient. I believe her. I am impressed she talked to the Uni and has made plans. And even more impressed she's made a note on her calendar about the next bill.

Therapist: And can you carry on having this discussion?

Helen: Well, I would be helped if you told me about the steps you are taking, or are planning to take to get more organized around finances. I could even help you think of ways if you wanted.

Rebecca: Okay, but you see, I am so behind you in this, I feel pretty stupid. I am like taking baby steps. I am like a stupid little girl in this.

Helen: No you're not. You're very clever. But you didn't grow up in a family that helped you think about these things so you are learning. Like I did, only in my family they taught us right from the start. But they didn't teach us about how to be joyful and how to be expressive. I'm learning that from you. Like a little girl!!

HOMEWORK TASKS/PRACTICING NEW FORMS OF COMMUNICATION

Homework tasks are ways people can try out, or practice new skills or insights from therapy at home. The therapist specifies the tasks as exactly as possible, getting agreement about when, where, and how. The therapist always makes sure that there is feedback from the couple on how the task went, or did not. It is important to say that there is no way to "fail": information about whether or not the task was helpful or whether or not it was even attempted is useful feedback. It can refine how a next step ought to be taken, or how to make any further tasks more constructive and useful.

- When appropriate, contract with either or both partners to refrain from specific behavior (for instance, behavior that has been agreed-upon as dangerous).

- Explore why behavioral agreements entered into by the partners have worked or failed to work, and reviewing goals in the light of this.

- Help couples identify and set their own goals.

- Establish the rules and procedures for achieving these goals.

EXAMPLE

Helen and Rebecca

Therapist: So I'm going to give you something to carry this on at home and then you can bring it back to our next appointment. It's practicing, in the real world, what you've been doing with me, here. And you can't "fail" because if for whatever reason it doesn't work, we just "fine-tune" it till it can work for you.

I know your mother's birthday, Helen, is coming up and your parents are coming down to London to have dinner with you both. Is there an issue you two can see arising that might cause the sort of argument we just saw you playing out? One where you both do your usual things, of Helen, looking calm but being very angry, and Rebecca becoming more overtly angry and then walking out, happens?

Rebecca: Yes, she's going to want me to dress very conservatively, all gray and white, and long skirts and low heels, and pull my hair back and not wear any makeup. She gets critical and all uptight whenever we see her family about how I look.

Helen: Yeah, that's right. And she doesn't want to make any adjustments to their feelings, to mine, about how they feel about our relationship and her difference from us in style at all. So, yeah, that's certainly one. Although last time it wasn't so bad. She didn't wear a low-cut red tight dress and her hair all over the place. I will give her that. (laughs)

Therapist: Okay. How about you stick to just one part of this: the color of the dress (or outfit) and what it means to each of you. Not to make a decision. But just to hear, each in turn, the pro of a somber one, for Helen, and a bright one for Rebecca. You would take turns to speak—one saying what the pro and con of your choice is, in turn, the other one listening. Then the other would simply reflect back what she'd heard, and the speaker would listen to make sure it was heard completely and correctly, saying what part might have been missing, and the listener saying back until it's completely checked out as correct. Then the other one goes. It's an active listening exercise, as we've done before. You'd have begun to appreciate, get an understanding of, what the feelings and issues are behind the way you dress for parents, for each of you, and you might then be able to go on to get to a better solution, eventually. It is a way to start, and I'd like you to try it, and it's practice in the skill of you listening to each other.

CULTUREGRAM

The culturegram is a diagram that provides a chance for intercultural couples to do some thinking about the differences in their family beliefs, values, traditions, and legacies. The culturegram can be used as a way of understanding and depicting family scripts (an intervention from the original EM). Family scripts are stories about how families ought to be, and roles within families, that are passed down from one generation to another. According to Byng-Hall (1985) family scripts could be replicative or corrective. When using a culturegram to investigate family scripts, the spokes depict the values and beliefs that are carried down over generations. The circle attached to the spoke could be thought of as replicative or corrective aspects of the family script.

The method is as follows:

- The therapist helps the couple to agree on a theme to focus on, for example, religious values.

- She then helps them draw a circle, and within the circle, write the answers to the following questions:

  - Where are you from?

  - What cultural and/or ethnic heritage do you identify with?

- Draw spokes. On each of these, write a belief or value about your theme that you picked up from the family you grew up in.

- In a circle attached to the end of each spoke, write about how the belief or value affects you now in your daily life (e.g., I go with it, I reject it, etc.).

- Compare and contrast your culturegram with that of your partner/supervisee.

EXAMPLE

Helen and Rebecca

In the case of Helen and Rebecca, a culturegram was used to explore gender and women's roles in each of their families of origin, and how these had been adapted in their relationship (see figure below).

In Helen's family, women were essentially homemakers, who did not for the most part work outside the house. Rebecca's mother is a doctor, and Rebecca came from a lineage of powerful, matriarchal women who had held jobs outside the home. Helen and Rebecca had thus inherited vastly different ideas about women's place outside their homes, from their families of origin. However, interestingly, in their own relationship (one coming from a replicative script and the other from a corrective script), they both valued professional achievement. They wondered how this affected roles in their relationship and in past ones.

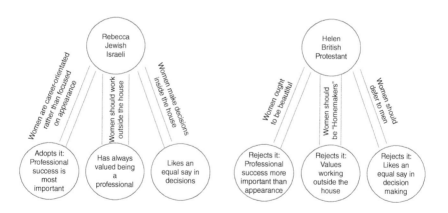

Systemic-Empathic Interventions

CHAPTER 8

Empathic Bridging Maneuvers

EMPATHIC QUESTIONING

These are interventions using types of interventions to create understanding, acceptance, tolerance, and empathic connections.

- Using empathic questioning to help the partners explore and reappraise their respective positions.

- Using questions, hypotheses, and/or reflections that can evoke emotions within the session in the service of then making them intelligible to each partner.

- Doing each of these within a "cultural frame"—that is, wondering if there is a connection to their respective ideas passed down through families and cultures—with reference to their genograms, culturegrams, and scripts—that need thinking through to see if there are different ideas and expectations that could be useful or are getting in the way.

EXAMPLE

Raja and Fiona

Therapist: It's really tough for you, Raja, when you see Fiona depressed. It must bring back for you the feeling you had when your mother was so ill when you were a boy, and your whole family was in an uproar: you thought she might die, you said. The fact that your grandparents came over from India must have really made you feel how serious that was, though you have said that that is very much what they would have done even if it hadn't been so serious, but you didn't know that for sure then. That must have been so frightening, especially as she went undiagnosed for so long, and was sick for so long.

The Intercultural Exeter Couples Model: Making Connections for a Divided World Through Systemic-Behavioral Therapy, First Edition. Janet Reibstein and Reenee Singh.
© 2021 John Wiley & Sons Ltd. Published 2021 by John Wiley & Sons Ltd.

Raja: Yeah, I think it does. I hadn't made that connection so clearly, but, yes, it makes me feel like I did then. I do feel like that. Very scared.

Therapist: I imagine, Fiona, that this connection might be new to you because Raja doesn't really talk about that as a time when he might have felt scared—even maybe depressed, himself—rather than angry or abandoned.

Fiona: No. He doesn't. So his reaction to me—I kind of see it a little differently now that you put it that way.

VALIDATION: USING INTERVENTIONS TO MAKE SOMEONE KNOW THEIR EXPERIENCES ARE UNDERSTANDABLE

• Responding empathically in order to validate the experience of each partner, especially their emotional experience.

• Validating and promoting acceptance of both existing and newly-experienced feelings of each partner.

EXAMPLE

Helen and Rebecca

Therapist: I wonder how you both felt when Rebecca had such a frightening allergic reaction to the hormones after your first try at *in vitro*? I imagine you both felt a lot of things: fear for Rebecca's health, of course, then maybe shock and disorientation. And sadness, frustration, even desperation or hopelessness. That's what anyone would feel. It is such an important thing, deciding to have a child, and then embarking with hope on trying to have one. It's something you are both so invested in, had done so much research over, spent so much time working out the way in which you wanted to try to have a child together, and spent a good deal of money over this, as well?

Helen: Well, I was really worried, but I didn't want Rebecca to know just how worried I was. She was really ill and I think she might have felt guilty that we'd decided she'd be the one to get pregnant and then she, her body, rejected the stuff you need to take to do the pregnancy. And she shouldn't feel like that, but I thought she might, so I just couldn't let her know how upset I was. Or all those other things. I think that's one reason I got so depressed, and had trouble talking about things.

Therapist: Yes—and that's sometimes what happens when you are overwhelmed by worry. It comes out in a different way, especially if you leave it inside and were taught differently about expressing things. I'm sort of surprised you don't say you two had arguments, for example. Sometimes the overwhelmed sense and the constant worry—they can come out that way.

Rebecca: We really didn't argue during that time. It was a bit weird—we were so calm, except I was sad and cried all the time. She was strong, not talking much like she's used to, and didn't, and I just thought she was taking it in her stride, again different from me.

> Therapist: You, yourself, must have been feeling like Helen was, too: overwhelmed, worried?
>
> Rebecca: But I didn't want to make her feel bad, by talking too much, so though I cried I didn't talk about the other stuff I was feeling. And I was feeling guilty and really, really desperate. Really overwhelmed, and really worried. We just sort of tried not to make the other one feel bad. So I knew she was concerned and worried. But I didn't want to say anything to her.
>
> Therapist: And sometimes people will feel, like you do, that it's best not to say anything or you'll make it worse, even though it might have made you feel more alone if you didn't talk.
>
> Rebecca: Yeah! But I think we maybe should have said something to each other because—yes, I think we wouldn't have felt so alone.

ELICITING VULNERABILITIES

These interventions bring people to the "softer" feelings so they can both connect, and empathize, and reveal difficult things they have felt or experienced to each other.

- Eliciting vulnerable feelings from each partner that may underlie their emotional reactions to their concerns.

- Encouraging them to express and elaborate these feelings.

- Conveying empathy and understanding for such feelings.

- Helping them to clarify when unexpressed emotional states might underlie expressed emotion (for instance when unexpressed fear underlies the expression of anger).

- Doing each of these within a "cultural frame"—that is, wondering if there is a connection to their respective ideas passed down through families and cultures—with reference to their genograms, culturegrams, and scripts—that need thinking through to see if there are different ideas and expectations that could be useful or are getting in the way.

EXAMPLE

Raja and Fiona

Raja: One of our major difficulties is around sex. Fiona just doesn't seem interested and I just think she doesn't fancy me. She gets annoyed and moody if I so much as touch her a lot of the time—she knows, or she immediately thinks that I am trying to see if she wants to have sex. And in my culture or family we don't talk about sex anyway.

Therapist: So I wonder if we could find out a little bit more about how you actually do feel when Raja touches you, for instance, Fiona. Raja says that you get annoyed, but I am wondering if there are other emotions that you are feeling, too?

Fiona: Umm... well, yes. I just feel sort of criticized. And pressured. And a little bit scared. Raja is always looking for clues that I fancy him. It's never enough.

Therapist: Ok. So it sounds like underneath the annoyance that Raja sees you are feeling criticized and frustrated that you can't be understood. And frightened, too, of something, though not sure why or what you are "frightened" about. Is that right?

Fiona: Yes. We don't talk easily about sex, but we do a bit so I expected him to ask.

Therapist: So that seems like it's really tough for you and hard to know what to do next about it...

MAKING LINKS BETWEEN VULNERABILITIES

- Helping partners empathically connect with each other by helping each partner develop empathy for the other's reactions through modeling empathy toward both partners.

- Helping the couple reach clearer shared understandings of each other's responses and meanings.

- Helping translate each partner's respective meanings of the other's behaviors.

- Encouraging the speaking partner to provide empathic feedback on their experience of being supported.

- Describing emotions in language that is both accessible and meaningful to the couple.

- Doing each of these within a "cultural frame"—that is, wondering if there is a connection to their respective ideas passed down through families and cultures—with reference to their genograms, culturegrams, and scripts—that need thinking through to see if there are different ideas and expectations that could be useful or are getting in the way.

EXAMPLE

(Continuing on with Raja and Fiona)

Therapist: So, Raja, is this cultural? This is slightly different from just "annoyed," though it probably also includes "annoyance"—if someone's frustrated and feels they're back in a loop that feels bad, they may become "annoyed" and that's what you'd see... but you see now that there's something there that's really quite painful—frightening—and I'm wondering if that leaves you feeling something like vulnerable

> Raja: It makes me sad. It makes me feel like I want to connect and I am lost, too; I am scared, too, because I feel rejected but I don't want to feel that I am making her feel bad, too. It makes me feel like we are both lost, lost souls, wanting to connect maybe but just not.... Again, we don't really talk 'emotions' in my family or culture, I guess.

CREATING SAFE SPACE

When working with the vulnerable "soft" feelings there needs to be a sense of safety within the room. These are interventions focused on creating this:

- Enhancing a sense of safety by encouraging each partner to talk first about low-level stressors that are removed from home before going on to talk about higher-level stressors that may be closer to home.

- Encouraging the speaking partner to identify what they might find helpful in coping with the stress.

- Enabling the listening partner to offer empathic support for the speaker in disclosing what they are finding stressful, and any specific needs they may have in order to cope with the stress.

- Using pacing and softening techniques to create safety in evoking emotion.

- Tuning into and validating emotional experience, for example by responding sensitively and robustly.

EXAMPLE

Fiona and Raja

Therapist: Let's start by exploring just your thoughts about going back to work, Fiona, before we talk about how and when you will start. We know that it might be difficult to talk about this particular thing, because you both have very different time frames for this, so we will come on to that later.

Fiona: Okay, but I'm afraid that when we talk about what I think about starting work again Raja is going to get all angry and start organizing me and telling me when to do what again.

Therapist (to Raja): How will we know that you are okay about hearing Fiona talk about how she feels about starting work again—that you are ready to hear her thoughts without getting anxious about how and when, because we know that's what has happened in the past?

Raja: When I know that she doesn't get all upset about the idea—doesn't start getting jumpy or closing me down or just shutting down and I can even mention it and it feels "normal."

Therapist: Raja has just named some of his anxieties about bringing up the subject—how he sees it makes you anxious. How can you let him know when it doesn't make you so anxious that it's safe even to begin to talk about this subject?

NORMALIZING

These are, like validation, making someone's experience feel understood; putting experience within the realm of "normality" and within what is "known" about how people behave, react, feel, and experience things.

- Making (and explaining when and why) emotional experience is usual, typical, expectable.

- Heightening awareness of the link between physiological arousal and emotional states (e.g., by using bio-feedback methods).

- Helping partners differentiate between their emotional states as experienced in themselves and as observed by others.

- Educating about emotional life and helping to label and define it.

- Doing each of these within a "cultural frame"—that is, defining things within a cultural frame: interrogating and defining any connections to their respective ideas passed down through families and cultures—with reference to their genograms, culturegrams, and scripts—to see if there are different ideas and expectations that could be useful or are getting in the way.

EXAMPLE

Rebecca and Helen

Helen: She drives me crazy. When she is late in her assignments and gets worried she gets completely messy and the house is just full of her papers and her books and then she gets completely preoccupied and forgetful. I go out to work all day and when I get home she hasn't done most of what needs to get done or she does them wrong even when I've written things down for her—she just doesn't seem to get it in her head right! And the dinner—she hasn't even thought about it; the lunch stuff—hers—is all over the table and dirty dishes in the sink. It's like she's just been sitting in in her study or in the kitchen feeding herself all day and nothing else matters. Before she began this intensive masters, she wasn't like this. She wasn't like this when we started. She was a bit messy, chaotic in some ways. But not like this.

Therapist: So it sounds like you feel very frustrated, Helen. I think that some of what you are describing are symptoms of the difference between you in your much more organized sort of approach to life, and how you were raised, and the culture—the boarding school, old-school British way of being very reliable and all of that. And then you are baffled when you come up against someone whose background is so entirely different, and whose culture values other things, and perhaps doesn't see disorganization as so terrible nor being so organized as such a virtue as your background and culture do. Under stress you might become super organized. Under stress Rebecca becomes less so. Some of that is temperament, some of that learning about how to organize yourself, some of that is cultural and familial and what you have both been taught within that and have come to value.

Rebecca: Yes, that sounds about right. When I'm like the way Helen describes it's because I am under unusual stress and my lack of organization skills fall apart while she gets even more so when she gets stressed. And we both need to learn about our differences. And I could use a bit more organizational skills. But she could also loosen up! That's what my culture can teach her!

TRANSLATING MEANING

These are interventions that link people through explicating meanings that might or might not be shared so they can be understood, even if different, or to explicate for them how meanings are, indeed, shared or overlap:

- Identifying and articulating relationship themes and meanings for each partner that lie behind specific behavior.

- Reframing the emotional experiences of partners to make them intelligible and acceptable to each other.

- Accepting and processing mismatches of emotional expression and responsiveness.

- Encouraging partners to "read" what their partner is thinking and feeling through:
  - picking up verbal and nonverbal cues and messages;
  - listening to feedback about the accuracy of these readings;
  - minimizing unhelpful "mindreading".

- Doing each of these within a "cultural frame"—that is, wondering if there is a connection to their respective ideas passed down through families and cultures—with reference to their genograms, culturegrams, and scripts—that need thinking through to see if there are different ideas and expectations that could be useful or are getting in the way.

EXAMPLE

Rebecca and Helen

Therapist: Helen, we know that Rebecca finds it difficult when you go to visit your family and your father makes remarks that she feels are a bit homophobic and that your parents do not really accept your relationship—you've discussed and argued about it many times. But what do you think she might be thinking and feeling right now, when you just told her you are going to your parents to visit this weekend?

Helen: I just know it seems like she really doesn't like my parents—she thinks a lot of what they think is covertly "homophobic" without really understanding that it's hard for them. They live in a small village, rural—you know: they didn't even think homosexuality existed there till like yesterday! And if they did it was all "just keep a stiff upper lip and don't let's say anything or discuss it." But then she seems to hate me for not standing up to them, not being all demonstrative and kissy-huggy around them, to make a "statement."

Therapist: Okay, so maybe "angry"? That's what you seem to be describing. What does Rebecca look like when she's "angry"?

Helen: Well, her face gets sort of twisted, and red, and she gets very loud and shouty.

Therapist: Does she look like that now?

Helen: No. No, she doesn't. I guess she looks a bit sad.

Therapist: Shall we check out with Rebecca if that's right? Shall we ask her if she hates your parents, or you when you don't stand up to them or show them that you love Rebecca?

Rebecca: Well, yes. Right now, and a lot—I do feel sad. I feel hurt because I don't feel I mean enough to Helen if she doesn't say something to her parents. I don't hate them. They're just scared, and ignorant. I understand why she's scared about doing anything that could upset them. I get it. But it makes me sad she won't take the chance. For me. For us.

Therapist: Are you surprised to hear that, Helen?

Helen: Sort of. Surprised she's not angry. Sort of surprised she's so sad more than that, I guess.

CIRCULAR QUESTIONING

Circular questions are ways of asking about situations indirectly, amassing information about the effects on, perspectives of, and positions around the others in a system. There are a range of these, which we show, below:

• Circular questions entail using different types of them to encourage new perspectives:

Types of Circular Questions

Circular questioning 1—Scaling Questions—for example:

Therapist: Can you tell me how you would rate this problem at the moment? If 0 was no problem at all and 10 was the worst it could possibly be, how would you rate things today? Can I ask you both this question?

Circular questioning 2—Future Orientated Questions—for example:

Therapist: So if the problem were to continue, what would things look like at home next month? ... And what about next year?

Circular questioning 3—Ranking Question—for example:

Therapist: Can you tell me how everyone else sees this problem at home? Let's rank everyone in terms of who you think the depression is the biggest problem for and who it is the least problem for ... so who is it the biggest problem for? And the next person? And the next?...

Circular questioning 4—New Alternative Questions—for example:

Therapist: So if the depression were to disappear overnight, what would that look like? If it was better, how would you know? What would I notice in therapy? What else would happen? Who else would be affected? Who else?

Circular questioning 5—Triadic Questions—for example:

Therapist: Can you tell me about Fiona and your mother's relationship, Raja? What does it look like to you? What do you notice?

Circular questioning 6—Outsider Observer Questions—for example:

Therapist: When the two of you are not getting on at home, if I was there as a fly on the wall, what would I notice?

Circular questioning 7—Self-Reflective on Self Questions—for example:

Therapist: How do you think this situation looks to Fiona? If you, Raja, were in Fiona's shoes, what would your behavior look like?

Circular questioning 8—Same Question Asked of All—for example:

Therapist: Can you tell me your thoughts about what happened last Tuesday night, Fiona? And what about yours, Raja?

Circular questioning 9—Contrast Questions—for example:

Therapist: So, can you tell me what things at home were like before Fiona became depressed? And how does that compare to now?

- Doing each of these within a "cultural frame"—that is, wondering if there is a connection to their respective ideas passed down through families and cultures—with reference to their genograms, culturegrams, and scripts— that need thinking through to see if there are different ideas and expectations that could be useful or are getting in the way.

EXTENDED EXAMPLE

Fiona and Raja

Therapist: So what do you think Fiona would say about that?

Raja: Well, I think she would say I don't help around the house enough... she might say I just sit around when she is home, that I leave her to try to look after the house and all, even when she is depressed....

Therapist: And your mum, who I gather is there a lot, so she is an onlooker, sort of? What would your mum be seeing?

Raja: I think my mum would be seeing that I am sitting around a lot. And she'd see Fiona doing all that stuff and she would see Fiona looking really pissed off. And she'd see that Fiona was nagging me. And she would think badly of Fiona as not a good wife.

Therapist: And if I were to ask Fiona to scale how big a problem it is for her that she wants you to help her more when she's depressed, and she feels you don't, how big would it be for Fiona, do you think, Raja? From 1 to 10, at this point? And why?

Raja: I'd say 10! For her, in her upbringing, husbands should be more helpful at home.

Therapist: And, Fiona? How big a problem do you think his "not helping you"—the thing that comes up as an argument so frequently between you when you have been depressed—is for Raja?

Fiona: About 1!

Therapist: So, Fiona, did Raja get it right for you? Is it 10?

Fiona: It used to be, but I think I understand a little bit more about how he thought it would actually help me when I got depressed—you know how in his family, in his culture, "working" is the answer, and he thought that that was like "working." I guess I think about it a little differently now, so it's about, say, 7 now.

Therapist: And Raja, did Fiona get the scaling right for you?

Raja: No. Not at all. I think it's about a 10 for me. I want to help and be different but I also am tired because I have been working out there, I mean in my job, and I don't want Fiona to think she's useless. So it's still about a 10 for me.

Therapist: So, Fiona, if depression were never going to happen again—let's say tomorrow you woke up and you knew that all the depression and everything around it were gone, what would it look like?

Fiona: I'd be out of bed, dressed and made up with no problem, helping get breakfast, making sure Raja was okay and seeing if he wanted a cup of coffee, for instance— all that, for a start!

BLAME REDUCTION

This is to get the couple to think about how they operate as a system, and ease them out of the "causality" model that attributes blame and guilt to a single person when there are problems, rather than looking at how problems are maintained through each one's actions and responses to each other. The interventions are about:

- Reducing blame, stimulating curiosity and encouraging empathy in the partners about their own and each other's perceptions.

- Through: "circular" questioning (questioning that highlights the interactive nature of each partner's behavior on the other).

- Doing each of these within a "cultural frame"—that is, wondering if there is a connection to their respective ideas passed down through families and cultures—with reference to their genograms, culturegrams, and scripts—that need thinking through to see if there are different ideas and expectations that could be useful or are getting in the way.

EXAMPLE

Fiona and Raja

Therapist: Fiona, what was Raja thinking or feeling, do you imagine, when you became depressed?

Fiona: I think Raja thought "When Fiona got ill the first time I was so worried. But I don't want to go through that all again! Is this what I married? Is this the way my life is going to go?"

Therapist: Raja, is he right?

Raja: Yes. I mean we told you, she was depressed once before and it was terrible, but that was I thought just because we'd moved and were far away from her best friend and her sister, and she didn't know anyone and mostly didn't have a job yet but I did and I was okay and all set but she wasn't. So when she got depressed again, I just was very scared about how we would cope. I thought this might be worse because now she did have friends here. But she didn't have a job, or not one that really was right for her yet. I was scared that she might never get one and if I was right, that she might always be like that—depressed or about to be depressed.

Therapist: So, Raja, was there anything this time that you noticed that might have been different, or did you think it was the same—her depression again. Was there anything different this time?

Raja: I think she was very worried this time about me and that I might just get too fed up with her. I was worried. And I got pretty down, myself.

Fiona: Well, yes. And I saw he was down because I was again. I noticed he was sliding down. But it just didn't seem fair!

Therapist: Do you think Raja noticed that you had noticed he was down? That's different from what he said about you being worried that he was fed up.

Fiona: No. He was too wrapped up in himself, I think. But maybe I couldn't see it because I was like that, myself.

Therapist: It sounds like such a hard time for you both! Like you both could have—and would have wanted to—support each other but couldn't do it?

Fiona: Yes, I think that's right. But I have been angry for a long time with Raja for him not being able to understand about depression and it's not just all about having a job and being the "right" sort of professional and that making it all okay, like it seems to be for his family! He is more right about it coming from a bunch of things—like not having close friends and family near. Or feeling you're worth anything. Some of that is about a job. Or working. But not all that much!

Therapist: Raja? What are you thinking about this?

Raja: I know she was—maybe still is—angry with me.

Therapist: I think you are both coming at this in different directions, from different perspectives. We've talked about this before: one family puts so much value and energy and importance into achievement through jobs and the other does not. One culture sees it through that lens, the other through a different one.

Fiona: Yes, and one makes you feel really guilty if you aren't a huge "success" and working all hours of the day to get ahead.

Raja: And one makes you feel guilty because you do that too much and don't see that you ought to be doing other stuff. Like, I don't know, going on walks—not something I ever did much when I was a kid or when I'd go to India to visit relatives. You don't go out on walks. Especially in the rain! So I feel guilty when I don't think about doing things like that and she feels I don't care because—I know now—she likes doing that.

Therapist: So "guilty" is about blame. I'm wondering if you still think in the same way of "blaming"?

Fiona: No, I think we put stuff on each other without thinking about what things mean to the other one. I'd like to do more walks, and I'd like to have the right job—both—because we each can shape the other one to do stuff differently.

Raja: I like that—it's not blame then, and not guilt—maybe about what can be good from what has shaped us so differently—that we can't help but bring different stuff, so we're not to "blame"—but we could use it differently, together?

CHAPTER 9

Life-Space Explorations

SCRIPTS

These are interventions that involve questions about what, how, and why people expect things of themselves and others, based on their family practices, beliefs, stories, and facts of their family lives. Scripts come into play at both large and small things—from transitions or traumatic or difficult times and also around what is expected behavior within the home, including gender roles or appropriate behavior. Scripts are also about how the blending of these two parts—the couple's individual scripts— how they interact and why, opening up avenues for a couple to question how they wish to be.

It involves:

- Taking a thorough family and relationship history for each partner, or facilitating this to emerge in the context of the therapeutic process, that includes attachment patterns, events, and themes—particularly in the light of cultural expectations.

- Reviewing how roles were allocated in previous partnerships and within families; focusing on role and gender expectations and expectations around crucial transitions and life events.

- Highlighting similarities and differences between each partner in terms of their familial and *cultural* expectations.

- Doing each of these within a "cultural frame"—that is, wondering if there is a connection to their respective ideas passed down through families and cultures—with reference to their genograms, culturegrams, and scripts— that need thinking through to see if there are different ideas and expectations that could be useful or are getting in the way.

The Intercultural Exeter Couples Model: Making Connections for a Divided World Through Systemic-Behavioral Therapy, First Edition. Janet Reibstein and Reenee Singh. © 2021 John Wiley & Sons Ltd. Published 2021 by John Wiley & Sons Ltd.

The notion of a "family script" was first set out clearly by Byng-Hall (1985) in which he describes how families create practices and set down expectations and norms that show family members what roles to play, and how to play them, in each situation, from how to behave and who does what at meals, to how to behave and who does what at major transitions, as well as what transitions to expect (e.g., marriage or not, births or not and, if so, at what age; work or not, and if so, what sort and by whom). Scripts will include gendered and culturally specific expectations about each. Byng-Hall pointed out that most clients instinctively understood the idea of "scripts" within families, making it a useful concept to employ within therapy. The "scripts" of how and why you do, or expect things are largely unconscious, so asking script questions can make the "unconscious conscious" and so allow a couple to make clearer and freer choices for themselves when scripts are articulated.

Scripts are also particularly used when doing culturegrams and cultural genograms (see below), as they each focus on cultural legacies that are often unconscious which come into play around big and small aspects of life. These will range, for instance, from conceptions of gender, to beliefs around both physical and mental illness and how to respond to it, to notions of how to conduct family life and bring up children, and beyond.

Investigating scripts also flows naturally from constructions of genograms (see below): extracting family scripts will tell how, why, and what do people get from their experiences of family life, handed down through generations.

EXAMPLE

Raja and Fiona

Therapist: So in your family of origin, Fiona, what were the beliefs about women's and men's roles in the family? Who was expected to do what?

Fiona: Well, it was a very traditional family. You know, women did the house stuff and men worked, and if women worked it was because we needed the money, but they could only do part-time, like my mum worked in the school a bit. That kind of thing.

Therapist: That sounds very different to your experience, Raja. Your mother worked all of your childhood, didn't she? And was a professional, wasn't she?

Raja: Yes, she was a doctor. And that was what was expected of both me and also my sister: to work and get good jobs. As well as to get married and have kids, of course.

Therapist: So that has meant you have different ideas about the meaning of jobs for all, but particularly for women.

GENOGRAM

This is a diagrammatic intervention that encapsulates quickly, easily and intelligibly family practices, beliefs, stories, and facts and shows, visually, each person's individual family in this way, making it possible to ask questions about how the individuals have been shaped. It is closely allied to asking about family scripts, but at its most basic, it is a visual depiction of who is in the family, who has been important to whom and why, who has been a problem to whom and why, and important facts about the family.

- Family genograms identify cross-generational family meanings, norms, and/or expectations, especially with regard to relationship roles and scripts.

- Genograms offer a tangible and graphic representation of complex family patterns (McGoldrick, Gerson & Shellenberger, 1999).

- The genogram is both an end product and a therapeutic process, moving focus away from the "identified patient" and toward wider questions about their context.

- The genogram in the IEM needs to include specific framing of questions to interrogate cultural ideas and practices: "Where did these come from?" "Do you think they represent ideas or beliefs that describe the background of your culture?" "Are these widely shared ideas or beliefs in the cultural community?" "Do you think that this thing that happened to X or Y in the genogram would be pretty typical of the culture?" "Do you think that that thing that happened or characterized X or Y in the genogram might be pretty typical for that culture or not?" etc. However, the cultural genogram extends and makes clearer graphically these questions (see the section on "Cultural Genogram," below).

A genogram is a pictorial depiction—a family tree—of the family, individual, or couple in therapy that sets out the person or people within generations and shows the links between people through marriage, cohabitation, and parenting. It displays continuities and discontinuities (deaths, break-ups; births, cohabitations, and marriages, for instance) and provides a display about which questions can be addressed, particularly around script issues (see section on "Scripts," above).

Fiona and Raja's genogram is as follows:

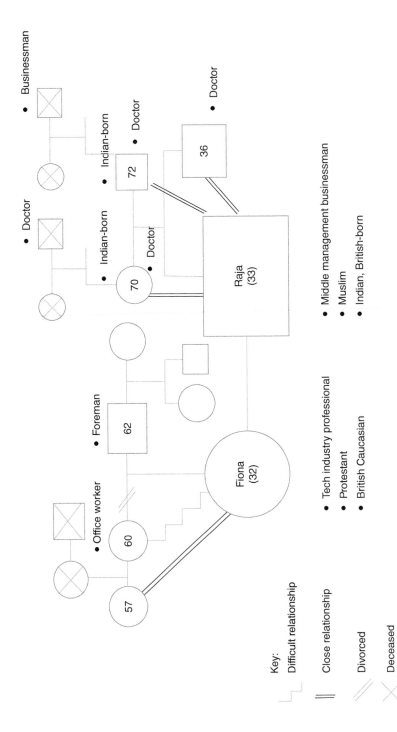

Businessman

Indian-born

Doctor

Doctor

Indian-born

Doctor

72

Doctor

36

Indian-born

Doctor

70

Raja
(33)

Foreman

62

Fiona
(32)

Office worker

60

57

- Middle management businessman
- Muslim
- Indian, British-born

- Tech industry professional
- Protestant
- British Caucasian

Key:
Difficult relationship

Close relationship

Divorced

Deceased

CULTURAL GENOGRAM

EXAMPLE

Helen and Rebecca

The cultural genogram is a method to expand the couple's stories and ability to question their often unspoken, differing and potentially conflictual cultural practices and beliefs. It can be used in conjunction with the IEM method of tracking the maintenance cycle of the interacting circularities: the thoughts and feelings part of which may well be informed by these differing yet unspoken beliefs and assumed practices. Vicious cycles have the possibilities to become virtuous cycles: adding in explicitly the intercultural dimension can unearth deeply held ideas and expectations that can block this process if not made clear.

In the case of a same sex couple, Helen, who is British Protestant, and Rebecca, who is Israeli Jewish, the couple began by choosing colors to represent their identities. Helen chose blue, and Rebecca chose red. As we drew a three generational family map or genogram, representing both sides of the family, we identified principles within the three generation family and issues of pride and shame (Hardy & Laszloffy, 1995). Thus, in Rebecca's family, being emotionally expressive was both an identifying principle or theme, as well as an issue of pride. On the other hand, Helen's family was far more reserved and to talk about feelings openly was frowned upon, and would have been seen as an issue of shame.

We explored the impact that these two differing belief systems, stemming from their family and cultural values, had on their interaction patterns. When upset and angry, Rebecca would scream and shout at Helen, who withdrew in response, which would make Rebecca even angrier. With the help of the IEM, we were able to help both Rebecca and Helen identify where these different styles came from, and to intervene at different stages of the cycle. For example, instead of shouting, Rebecca was coached to explain how she felt to Helen, who learned how to listen, instead of withdrawing and physically leaving the room.

INTERVIEWING INTERNALIZED OTHER

This is an intervention that encourages empathic connection. It asks the one to try to "be" the other, living in the shoes of the other, as he or she is asked questions "as" the other. It goes further than role-playing, as the person within the interview is answering fully in the experience of being the other, rather than as an observer of them.

- Individually interviewing each member of a pair, inviting them to speak as the inner voice of the other (Tomm, 1998).

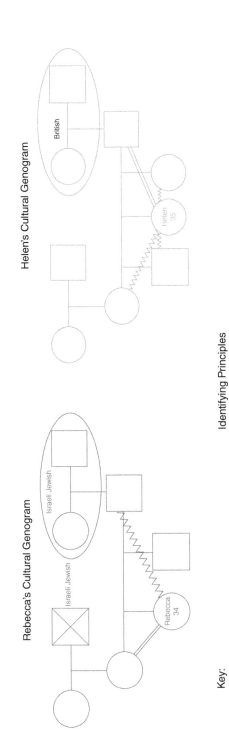

Rebecca's Cultural Genogram

Israeli Jewish

Israeli Jewish

Rebecca
34

Helen's Cultural Genogram

British

Helen
35

Identifying Principles

Rebecca – emotions should be expressed	Helen – reserved, it is not right to talk about how you feel

Key:

Israeli Jewish on the left-Rebecca

British on the right-Helen

☐ Deceased

⊠ Deceased

// Strong Bond

᭒ Conflict

᭒ Close & conflictual

- Interviewing each person as the other in the couple ensuring to set up the interview with orientating questions first and de-role at the end of the interview.

EXAMPLE

Rebecca and Helen

Rebecca (as Helen): I'm 35.

Therapist: And your family, Helen? Do you have siblings? Parents? Can you tell me their names?

Rebecca (as Helen): Yes, I have two brothers, Joe and James. James is married and has a baby son. Joe lives in Darlington with his girlfriend.

Therapist: And your parents? Are they in London, like you and Rebecca, Helen?

Rebecca (as Helen): No, no. They live in Derbyshire in a small village. They're Sue and Jimmy.

Therapist: Okay. That's interesting. So, Helen, your brother is named for your father, is that right?

Rebecca (as Helen): Yeah. James Jr. But he's never called Jimmy. But, yeah, that's important. My dad is, well, he's sort of like a dictator in the family.

Therapist: But, Helen, Rebecca has said that he is different with you. That you are—she said—his "angel." Is she right? Do you feel like you are his "angel?"

Rebecca (as Helen): Yeah. She's right. He is different with me. He's a lot gentler.

Therapist: So is that comfortable being his angel?

Rebecca (as Helen): Well, sometimes. But sometimes it isn't.

Therapist: Can you say which times it isn't?

Rebecca (as Helen): When I know that he wouldn't approve of things that his "angel" shouldn't be doing?

Therapist: Can you give me an example?

Rebecca (as Helen): Well, obviously, he wouldn't approve of me being in a same-sex relationship!

Therapist: And you know that for sure?

Rebecca (as Helen): Oh, yes! He's like, he's like, well anything that's not just like the "normal" and what he understands is like, well, the enemy, the worst to him. And that's what that village is like: it's not "normal" to be like me and Rebecca!!

Therapist: So, Helen, that must make you feel terrible. What a bind! When he does that what happens inside to you?

Rebecca (as Helen): I just hurt so badly. I just feel so terrible. And I know that just going silent is terrible. I know that...

Therapist:

Ok, Helen. Thank you. That was really helpful to hear from you.

But now I want to see Rebecca again.

So Rebecca, can I ask you, now—you are Rebecca—to stand up, and take another seat, first. Okay?

Rebecca stands up and takes another seat.

Therapist: Okay, Rebecca, now I want you to say who you are, and in one way you are not Helen.

Rebecca: I am Rebecca. I am not 35 years old. I am 34. And I have brown curly hair and Helen has long straight hair, not as dark as mine is. I am Jewish. Helen is Catholic, although I know we're both not really that.

Therapist: How was it for you being Helen, Rebecca? Comfortable or not? Do you think you learned or felt anything new?

Rebecca: Actually it was surprisingly comfortable. I felt I could feel like Helen and sometimes I don't feel like I can because I get so angry with her. But I felt really bad for her when I talked about her father. Really sort of welled-up—it must be awful for her!

Therapist: Thank you. That's really interesting—and that is why we do this exercise: to get into how it feels to be the person we love and want to know better. Now (turning to Helen): How was it for you hearing yourself through Rebecca? Did Rebecca have "you" right? Or in some ways "right" and others not?

ATTACHMENT NARRATIVES

These are interventions that explore the early and historical emotional attachments and feelings or not of security and trust that have come about as a result, including childhood ones that form the basis, and later emotional attachment histories that have cemented or not—changing in some direction or not—the early ones, that affect and have affected the interactions within the current relationship through:

DEVELOPING SHARED FORMULATIONS OF CENTRAL RELATIONSHIP THEMES

- Exploring the transference of representations of past attachment patterns, roles, and affects into current couple and/or therapy relationships, and helping the couple distinguish between past and present meanings and realities.

- Helping clients to understand, mourn, leave in their place past attachment difficulties, disappointments, and losses.

- Helping clients to make accessible and accepting feared emotions/experiences, and encouraging new ways that partners can be with each other.

- Helping clients to provide the context for a corrective emotional experience that encourages each partner to feel secure with each other.

- Working with mismatches between partners' emotional responses and meanings, for example by building awareness between partners of their different attitudes, histories, and experiences with expressing specific emotions or:

- Building awareness between partners of their different attitudes toward introspection, self-disclosure, and exploration of feelings.

- Doing each of these within a "cultural frame"—that is, wondering if there is a connection to their respective ideas passed down through families and cultures—with reference to their genograms, culturegrams, and scripts— that need thinking through to see if there are different ideas and expectations that could be useful or are getting in the way.

EXAMPLE

Fiona and Raja

Therapist: So can you tell me, Fiona, what your previous relationships were like? Did you struggle with depression in your previous relationship, the one you were in before you met Raja?

Fiona: Yes, I guess I've always been a little like this... I was Daddy's girl, but then Daddy left when I was a teenager and I guess I've always thought people would leave me, like I wasn't really worth them staying or I wasn't good enough for them to stay. It's probably all down to that and also that my mother got very depressed and she just wasn't there. She was in hospital. And I never got along with her anyway—she knew I was Daddy's and I never felt she wanted me, either. And then she'd slag off my father after he left for leaving her and that made me mad. I mean they had a terrible relationship. Always rowing.

Therapist: So it sounds like you are saying that your experience of your mother, for instance, as a young person, was that she didn't make you feel like she wanted you, and then your father who did, then left you and you felt like you weren't important enough for him to want to stay with you, either.

Fiona: Yeah, that's about it.

Therapist: So did you think that if you were different somehow, that your father would have stayed? Or something like that? Or if you were somehow different your mother would have shown you more love?

Fiona: Yeah. I think it is something that I'm just not enough or something like that.

Therapist: So do you assume that Raja also feels like that about you? That if you were somehow "more" in some way, or maybe "better" you'd feel more sure he wanted to be with you? Do you think you are bringing those ideas from childhood into now?

Fiona: Yeah, I suppose I do think that. Especially since he has always pushed me to "achieve" and his family keeps looking for me to do that. Like they do.

Therapist: So, let's think, Fiona. When you were little and you had bad feelings about yourself like that, for instance, when your dad left, or when your mum slagged him off, or when she said anything that made you feel she didn't really want you, did you turn to anyone when you were upset, or when you might have been scared by things she said or when he left? Was there anyone?

> Fiona: I used to with my dad when he was around which wasn't so much. But when he left, I used to talk a bit to my auntie, his sister, who lived near us and she used to come around. She was a lot younger and she'd babysit sometimes. But then she stopped because my mum and she didn't get along. So that's when I began to hang around with that crowd—you know, started to drink and stuff.
>
> Therapist: So with your boyfriend before Raja, the one you lived with for a while. Did you feel the same with him?
>
> Fiona: Oh, yeah, for sure. But not at first. At first he was like, you are so wonderful, all that. But yeah, he was terrible! He just used to say terrible things to me, do terrible things, not like Raja, not at all. But yeah, for sure.

RECONCEPTUALIZING THE POSITIVES

These are the opposite of "pathologizing" maneuvers: they are to show the positives within the repertoire of experiences and behaviors that already exist and that can be built upon, showing the possibilities for positives.

- Reconceptualizing a partner's perceived negative motivations as misguided or misfired attempts to be supported by and/or supportive of the other.

- Emphasizing the desire of partners to enable rather than disable each other.

- Doing each of these within a "cultural frame"—that is, wondering if there is a connection to their respective ideas passed down through families and cultures—with reference to their genograms, culturegrams, and scripts—that need thinking through to see if there are different ideas and expectations that could be useful or are getting in the way.

EXAMPLE

Raja and Fiona

Fiona: When things are difficult, like when I've got really stressed and unhappy and get depressed, and Raja just sees that I am not coping and feeling terrible, when things get like that, he calls his mum. He has told her about my medication and my feeling so low. And don't get me wrong, I do love his mum and dad, but I really don't appreciate her telling me that if I just got up and out and made things happen and pushed myself I'd just be all fine and dandy. Giving me her sort of "pep talks." And she's a doctor, so they talk about my medication which I think is interfering.

Therapist: I wonder if we could think about Raja's conversations with his mum as their discussions as "caring," rather than interfering, though you'd show "caring" perhaps in a different way to them. I'm wondering if it means that Raja and also his mum are worried about you? Are doing what they think would help them if they were like that—at least that they think would help them!

Fiona: Yeah, I can see that. I suppose so. I know he cares. That is for sure: he cares for me. And even his mum does.

Therapist: So maybe you and Raja, Fiona, can have a conversation now—now that you can see it as caring rather than "interfering"—about "caring" when you are worried and how it can work better between the two of you?

Fiona: Yeah. Yeah, sure. I don't want him to be worried.

Raja: But I do want to care, and to show you that I do. But so you would recognize it as "caring" not "pressuring."

CREATING SHARED POSITIVES

These are interventions that encourage the couple to take a positive shared perspective on their relationship, to focus on their attempts to change toward positivity and constructive interacting. They include:

• Encouraging partners to talk to each other about respective hopes and fears they have about their relationship, especially when they feel upset or threatened.

• Establishing and noting, to underline their intentional nature, the partners' daily rituals of connecting with each other (over meal times, shared activities, and so on).

• Identifying ways, and noting their intentional nature, in which partners already are supported by each other in their shared roles (parenting, home maintenance, and so on).

• Facilitating the emergence and recognition of a shared relationship story: noting how it clarifies and sustains the values and meanings the partners have in common.

• Doing each of these within a "cultural frame"—that is, wondering if there is a connection to their respective ideas passed down through families and cultures—with reference to their genograms, culturegrams, and scripts— that need thinking through to see if there are different ideas and expectations that could be useful or are getting in the way.

EXAMPLE

Fiona and Raja

Therapist: So, for you two, Fiona and Raja, it sounds as if you have some new understandings of how to manage your differences if and when Fiona might feel low again?

Raja: Well, I know that she doesn't find it "caring" to pep talk her into thinking her job is the answer and to get up and just stop feeling bad. I think I understand more that she just wants me to be there for her, and to make her feel I'm thinking of her as someone who is loveable and let her feel that...

Fiona: That's right—so I won't feel useless. But I think I understand a bit more that actually it does make me feel better if I am doing something but if Raja doesn't think that's the only thing that matters or is worthwhile—working, doing, all that—I could do more of that!

Therapist: So what is it that you could be doing more of to make you both keep some of these things in mind, especially now that Fiona isn't so depressed and you can see forward a bit better?

Fiona: Well, I think we could take some more walks. Even in the rain...

Raja: Yeah, but also I'm happy to not work so much. I was actually worried she'd never work again, and I was working so hard to get noticed and promoted and crazily working... I guess we understand a bit more about who we are and how we got to be that way. My way isn't the only way. Hers has lots of good stuff in it, too. I got Wellies, by the way. My first proper pair.

CHAPTER 10

A Final Word

The Therapist's Experience in Intercultural Couples Work

Thus far, we have outlined the theoretical tenets of the Intercultural Exeter Model. We have unpacked and explored the interventions of the model, illustrated through our work with two intercultural couples—Raja and Fiona, and Helen and Rebecca.

Perhaps the one thing missing from the descriptions is a focus on how the work affects *us*—the clinicians working with this model—and how in turn, our responses and the positions we take have an impact on the work.

Part of this means asking how do we position ourselves as psychotherapists, working with intercultural couples? Falicov (2014) suggests that the clinical encounter with an intercultural couple requires the clinician to be self-reflexive about their own culture and cultural values. This is of course because one of our most important tools as clinicians is the use of our own self reflexivity. By this we mean how we experience what is going on in the session, including what personal resonances the material and emotional states summon in us, the sense we can make of this, the emotional control we can manage over them, and the creative, constructive and fruitful use we can make of our self-reflectivity for our clients. Whilst this is important in working with any couple, the system that is created when working with intercultural couples means we have to be particularly alive to the *culturally-based* resonances for us, personally. For the therapeutic encounter in such work means that it comprises three cultures: that of each of the partners and the one of the therapist, thus increasing the possibilities for cultural alliances, splits, and misunderstandings.

When working with Helen and Rebecca, for example, RS, herself a native-born Indian who emigrated to the UK, could relate to the fact that Rebecca's family were migrants from Israel, and that she identified as being from a minority ethnic group. RS used her own experiences of emigration to help Helen to make sense of Rebecca's family's experiences of holding on to aspects of their own culture and religion. She also drew on her own experiences of racism in the UK as a member of a minority group to explore Rebecca's experiences of anti-semitism. In doing so, though, she had to be careful not to ally herself so closely to Rebecca that the therapeutic alliance with Helen would become threatened. The handling of this clinical dilemma is illustrative of an aspect of both the strengths—the ability to empathize and identify—and pitfalls—the imbalance resulting from such identification—of using the self in intercultural couples work. Of course, in therapy, quite beyond the intercultural dimension, other circumstances will resonate and call on the need for self-reflexivity. For example, RS is someone who prides herself on being organized and tidy so she used this to understand Helen's frustration with Rebecca's mess and chaos. One can use one's resonances and understandings, of course, implicitly—one does not need to explicitly share either similarities and differences of one's own stories with this couple, although the sparing use of experience as illustrations with their clinical usefulness made explicitly can be useful. Using experiences in the work with Helen and Rebecca did help create a vital therapeutic bridge.

Similarly, JR, herself, an émigré from the US to the UK, married to a British citizen, also from a different religion, used her own experience of raising British sons of an émigré to understand Raja's position as a son caught in the midst of two cultures. What felt frustrating to Fiona about Raja's adherence to his parents' and grandparents' cultural expectations around work and about depression, in particular, resonated with her as she remembered similar conversations with one of her grown sons, and the different expectations particularly around expressiveness between, first, his own parents, and now, between him—as he came to realize that he had adopted more than he'd known from his American heritage—and his British partner. Similarly, as with RS and her work with Helen and Rebecca, there were other moments of identification beyond the intercultural ones. A case in point was when Raja mentioned his own mother's illness when he was a child. In that case, JR did offer a personal experience of having been the child of an ill mother. The explicit purpose in doing so was to explore the many potential ways, mediated by culture, in which children understand a parent's incapacitation, to open up a discussion with them about the cultural ways in which children are given permission or not to talk about their feelings. The American, British, and Indian ways were all, therefore, brought in to think about, and to give this couple more degrees of freedom in which to think about and react to, Fiona's "illness" of depression.

Burnham and his colleagues (2008) devised the acronym the Social *GGRRAAACCEEESSS* (standing for gender, race, religion, age, ability, class, culture, ethnicity, education, sexuality, and spirituality (as well as geography, employment, sexual orientation, and spirituality) to describe the interplay between aspects of difference. Burnham (2012) expands this idea to discuss GGRRAAACCEEESSS that are visible, invisible, voiced, or unvoiced. The social GGRRAAACCEEESSS are a useful way of thinking about how differences both between intercultural couples and between the couples and the therapist can be conceptualized. The main differences between RS and Rebecca and Helen were sexual orientation and age. RS was transparent about being a heterosexual, older woman, and would often ask questions about these invisible, but voiced aspects of our difference from a position of respectful curiosity (Dyche & Zayas, 1995), for instance: one example was when Helen was talking about the difficulties in "coming out" as a gay woman to her parents. RS drew on, and shared her experiences of speaking to her parents about wanting to marry somebody from a different culture, but also acknowledged that, as a heterosexual woman, she did not have any personal experiences of the complicated process of "coming out" to one's family and friends. She recognized, as well, that, although there may be some universal themes, this process was probably quite culturally different for Helen and Rebecca. She thought with them about intersectionality; about how culture could impact on the experiences of coming out and reflected as she did, out of her position as a South Asian woman, about how particularly complicated this process would be for lesbian women in South Asian communities.

But in contrast, the therapist might be visibly similar to one partner within an intercultural couple, giving rise to expectations of identification where that assumed similarity might not really exist. A multitude of unvoiced differences can exist behind seeming sameness, whether from class, particularity of experience and timing of migration in the case of transplantation, or of closeness to others from one's family or relatives or their expectations of adherence to cultural ideas and practices, or differences of class, age, or other of the GRRAACCEESS. For instance, in the following example, RS as a South Asian worked with an intercultural couple where the female partner was Bangladeshi. RS was visibly similar to her client. However, in that case the differences between them in age, class, and religion were numerous, and things we had to bridge; RS in fact, based on other similarities of experience, was more able to identify with the experiences of the White British male partner. Indeed, Burnham's framework helped unpack the complexities and nuances of further difference, as well as similarities, in this couple's work with RS.

Moreover, work with this and many other intercultural couples was—and should be—helped by thinking clearly about notions of Whiteness and White privilege (Wallis & Singh, 2014) in order to help couples to understand the difference in the power dynamics within them, as discussed in Chapter 4. Another helpful, although non-clinical, text that argues for a continual consciousness of White privilege and its continuous seepage into the lives of both White and non-White lives, making experience always different and always hierarchical, is De Angelo's influential book, *White Fragility* (2018), or, from the position of a Black woman's experience, Eddo-Lodge's—*Why I'm No Longer Talking to White People about "Race"* (2017). To dismiss this fact is to misunderstand people's lived experience and to silence non-White voices. Thus, by becoming conscious and knowing safe ways of speaking openly about the vexed issues of "race" and racism, a couple, themselves, can find ways to do so and honor and understand their experience, as the therapist can, as well.

Throughout this book we have demonstrated that the visual and representational methods of the cultural genogram and culturegram, in particular, and forming questions, within the other interventions, that make the couple have to unearth intercultural ideas and practices and examine how these have shaped their lives, can prove fruitful and enlightening for intercultural couples. Although the Intercultural Exeter Model's interventions are largely posited upon an evidence base, there are emerging interventions, whose evidence base remains yet unestablished but whose clinical, anecdotal use show promise that, if similarly pointed toward intercultural questions could be useful. These include positioning lines, sculpts, and emotion maps (Gabb & Singh, 2015a) and the use of drawings (Singh, 2017), as might an intervention imported from Killian's (2013) work. He uses the idea of "universalising the particular" to demonstrate how an interaction between a couple can be linked to happenings in the wider sociopolitical context—which obviously can mean easily bringing in intercultural issues explicitly. For example, a row over one parent's overprotectiveness in a dual-heritage family can be related to recent media coverage of racist attacks in the family's neighborhood—and so it can offer the opening of a conversation about race and its role within the couple. With this work, however, comes its other side: stereotyping. As therapists we need to be exquisitely mindful of stereotyping from the universal and thus dehumanizing our clients, and to the stereotyping from the universal that can come from our clients. Hearing, as one of us has, from a client the statement, "this is what White men are like," with its stereotyping from the universal, and being alive to this possibility, we were able to usefully deconstruct and examine it within the context of that couple's particular histories and beliefs.

Falicov's (2016) perspective is that an interactional couple's interactions are inevitably affected by sociopolitical and economic inequalities, as societies are inevitably structured hierarchically by things that include a hierarchy in which certain cultures (the dominant one, in particular) sit above others. The couples are, of course, also inevitably affected by the sorts of things we have spent much of this book pointing to: values, practices, and beliefs. Moreover, though, Falicov says the inevitability of the complexity of work with intercultural couples means that there is also a hierarchy of these very things, themselves: certain beliefs, values, and practices are supposed to be "right" or "better" because they are the dominant ones. Consciousness of this when you work with intercultural couples, for a therapist, along with the consciousness, as we have said, of race, is part of the process of self-reflexivity we have been discussing. Systemic practitioners are trained to intervene at the level of process, but when working with intercultural couples, we have to be mindful also of the level of content—that of the beliefs, practices, and ideas. But not just what it means for the couple and their interactions, also for us. For example, cultural differences in values and beliefs which are related to parenting, or religion, or language or food will have a resonance for our own about these. We need also to be thoughtful about the socioeconomic and power differences inevitably produced within the couple by these very things. Mindfulness of these is not just awareness of them, per se, that is, but also of our own assumptions and feelings about these hierarchies of content and power.

But there is also the other side which we, as therapists cannot forget. Again, Falicov, who has written much and long about intercultural work, highlights this important caveat: that we must not assume that every intercultural couple will have difficulties nor that every difficulty between them is intercultural in nature (Falicov, 2016). When intercultural couples come to see us at the London Intercultural Couples Centre we try to keep a frame in mind that they are bringing to us a richness: a variety of thinking, acting, and believing that can open our minds and that can bring creativity as much as difficulty to their lives. The mere fact that clients are seeking out such a specialist service could mean that they are reifying "intercultural" differences as "difficulties." It could mean that they have lost sight of the fact that difference had been a feature of what made them drawn to each other in the first place, and that they have lost their way in negotiating an interesting and varied way of living together as they've stumbled over the complexity of their differences. It is our task, and the task of therapists who work with this growing phenomenon of intimate life within cultural differences, to remember that it is not just about growth and help toward a better life for the couples who come to us, but also to a larger growth within the world. That is, of the richness of change that blending people's lives can mean. We hope our book, through guiding therapists through intercultural couples work, can help therapists help couples think about lives in that way. At our Centre we try to do this by highlighting the complex interplay between culture, gender, religion, and class, and also by trying to find and foreground the resiliencies and strengths of the intercultural couple relationships with which we are honored to work.

References

Baucom, D., Whisman, M. A., & Paprocki, C. (2012). Couple-based interventions for psychopathology. *Journal of Family Therapy*, *34*(3), 250–270.

Berlin, R., & Cannon, H. (2013). *Mixed blessings: A guide to multicultural and multiethnic relationships*. Seattle, WA: Mixed Blessings, LLC.

Berman, P. (1968). *A tale of two utopias. The political journey of the generation of 1968*. New York: W.W. Norton and Company.

Bhugra, D., & De Silva, P. (2000). Couple therapy across cultures. *Sexual and Relationship Therapy*, *15*(2), 183–192. doi:10.1080/14681990050010763

Bhugun, C. D. (2017). *The experience of intercultural parenting in Australia* (PhD dissertation). Southern Cross University, Australia.

Burck, C. (2005). Comparing qualitative research methodologies for systemic research: The use of grounded theory, discourse analysis and narrative analysis. *Journal of Family Therapy*, *27*(3), 237–262.

Burnham, J., Alvis Palma, D., & Whitehouse, L. (2008). Learning as a context for differences, and differences as a context for learning. *Journal of Family Therapy*, *30*, 529–542.

Burnham, J. (2012). Developments in the social GRRRAAACCEEESSS. Visible-invisible and voiced-unvoiced. In I. B. Krause (Ed.), *Culture and reflexivity in systemic psychotherapy* (pp. 139–160). London, UK: Karnac.

Byng-Hall, J. (1985). *The family script: A useful bridge between theory and practice. Journal of Family Therapy*, *7*(3), 301–305.

Bystydzienski, J. M. (2011). *Intercultural couples: Crossing boundaries, negotiating difference*. New York, NY: New York University Press.

Caballero, C., Edwards, R., & Puthussery, S. (2008). *Parenting 'mixed' children: Negotiating difference and belonging in mixed race, ethnicity and faith families*. Joseph Rowntree Foundation. Retrieved August 15, 2011, from https://www.researchgate.net/profile/Chamion_Caballero/publication/265537866_Parenting_'Mixed'_Children_Difference_and_Belonging_in_Mixed_Race_and_Faith_Families/links/54b911660cf28faced626ac3.pdf

Cadenhead, R.A. (2018) *How is culture talked into being in intercultural couple therapy?* (Unpublished dissertation. Masters in Family Therapy). Institute of Family Therapy, London.

The Intercultural Exeter Couples Model: Making Connections for a Divided World Through Systemic-Behavioral Therapy, First Edition. Janet Reibstein and Reenee Singh.
© 2021 John Wiley & Sons Ltd. Published 2021 by John Wiley & Sons Ltd.

Crippen, C. (2008). *Cross-cultural parenting: Experiences of intercultural parents and constructions of culturally diverse families* (Unpublished doctoral dissertation). University of New England, Australia.

Crippen, C. (2011). *Working with intercultural couples and families: Exploring cultural dissonance to identify transformative opportunities*. Retrieved June 20, 2012 from https://www.counseling.org/resources/library/vistas/2011-V-Online/Article_21.pdf

Crowe, M., & Ridley, J. (1990). *Therapy with couples*. London, UK: Blackwell.

Davis, K. (1941). Intermarriage in caste societies. *American Anthropologist, 43*, 388–395.

De Angelo, R. (2018). *White fragility*. New York, NY: Beacon Press.

Dyche, L., & Zayas, L. (1995). *The value of curiosity and naivete' the cross-cultural psychotherapist. Family Process, 34*(4), 389–399.

Eddo-Lodge, R. (2017). *Why I'm no longer talking to white people about 'race.'*. London, UK: Bloomsbury.

Falicov, C. J. (1995). Cross-cultural marriages. In N. Jacobson & A. Gurman (Eds.), *Clinical handbook of couple therapy* (2nd ed., pp. 231–246). New York, NY: Guilford Press.

Falicov, C. J. (2014). *Latino families in therapy* (2nd ed.). New York, NY: Guilford Press.

Falicov, C.J. (2016). *Intercultural couples*. Plenary Presentation. European Family Therapy Association conference, Athens.

Forry, N. D., Leslie, L. A., & Letiecq, B. L. (2007). Marital quality in interracial relationships: The role of sex role ideology and perceived fairness. *Journal of Family Issues, 28*, 1538–1552.

Fowers, B. J., & Olson, D. H. (1993). ENRICH marital satisfaction scale: A reliability and validity study. *Journal of Family Psychology, 7*, 176–185.

Gabb, J., & Singh, R. (2015a). The uses of emotion maps in research and clinical practice with families and couples: Methodological innovation and critical inquiry. *Family Process, 54*, 185–197.

Gabb, J., & Singh, R. (2015b). Reflections on the challenges of understanding racial, cultural and sexual differences in couple relationship research. *Family Process, 37*(2), 210–227.

Gaines, S. O., & Brennan, K. A. (2001). Establishing and maintaining satisfaction in multicultural relationships. In H. Harvey & A. Wenzel (Eds.), *Close romantic relationships: Maintenance and enhancement* (pp. 237–253). Mahwah, NJ: Lawrence Earlbaum Associates.

Garcia, D. R. (2006). Mixed marriages and transnational families in the intercultural context: A case study of African-Spanish couples in Catalonia. *Journal of Ethnic and Migration Studies, 32*(3), 4.

Gilbert, P. (2010). *Compassion focused therapy: Distinctive features*. London, UK: Routledge.

Gottman, J. (1994). *Why marriages succeed or fail: And how you can make yours last*. New York, NY: Simon and Schuster.

Gottman, J., Notarius, C., Gonso, J., & Markman, H. (1976). *A couple's guide to communication*. London, UK: Routledge.

Gurung, R. A. R., & Duong, T. (1999). Mixing and matching: Assessing the concomitants of mixed-ethnic relationships. *Journal of Social and Personal Relationships, 16*(5), 639–657. doi:10.1177/0265407599165005

Hafner, R. J., Badenoch, A., Fisher, J., & Swift, H. (1983). Souse-aided vs individual therapy in persisting psychiatric disorders: A systematic comparison. *Family Process*, *21*(3), 227–237.

Hardy, K., & Laszloffy, T. A. (1995). The cultural genogram: Key to training culturally competent family therapists. *Journal of Marital and Family Therapy*, *21*(3), 227–237.

Hayes, S. C., Luoma, J. B., Bond, F. W., Masuda, A., & Lillis, J. (2006). Acceptance and commitment therapy: Model, processes and outcomes. *Behaviour Research and Therapy*, *44*, 1–25.

Heller, P., & Wood, B. (2000). The influence of religious and ethnic differences on marital intimacy: Intermarriage versus intramarriage. *Journal of Marital and Family Therapy*, *26*, 241–252.

Herr, G. J. (2009) *Factors influencing black-white interracial marriage satisfaction.* (Unpublished doctoral dissertation). The University of Texas at Arlington. Retrieved August 22, 2018 from http://citeseerx.ist.psu.edu/viewdoc/download?doi=10.1.1.626.8764&rep=rep1&type=pdf

Hibbler, D. K., & Shinew, K. J. (2017). Interracial couples' experience of leisure: A social network approach. *Journal of Leisure Research.*, *34*(2), 135–156.

Ho, M. K. (1990). *Intermarried couples in therapy.* Springfield, IL: Charles C. Thomas.

Hsu, J. (2001). Marital therapy for intercultural couples. In W. S. Tseng & J. Streltzer (Eds.), *Culture and psychology: A guide to clinical practice* (pp. 225–242). Washington, DC: American Psychiatric Publishing.

Irastorza, N., & Devoretz, D. (2009). *Factors affecting international marriage survival: A theoretical approach.* Retrieved January 15, 2016 from http://www.sfu.ca/~devoretz/lecturenotes/sem9.pdf

Jacobson, N. S., & Christenson, A. (1998). *Acceptance and change: A therapist's guide to transforming relationships.* New York, NY: W. W. Norton.

Jacobson, N. S., & Margolin, G. (1979). *Marital therapy: Strategies based on social learning and behaviour exchange principles.* New York, NY: Brunner and Mazel.

Johnson, S., Bradley, B., Furrow, J. L., Lee, A., Palmer, G., Tilley, D., & Woolley, S. (2005). *Becoming an emotionally-focused couple therapist.* London, UK: Taylor and Francis.

Jones, E., & Asen, E. (2000). *Systemic couple therapy and depression.* London, UK: Karnac Books.

Kenney, K., & Kenney, K. (2012). Contemporary multiple heritage couples, individuals and families: Issues, concerns, and counselling implications. *Counselling Psychology Quarterly*, *25*(2), 99–112.

Killian, K. D. (2001a). Reconstituting racial histories and identities: The narratives of interracial couples. *Journal of Marital and Family Therapy*, *27*, 23–37.

Killian, K. D. (2001b). Crossing borders: Race, gender and their intersections in interracial couples. *Journal of Feminist Family Therapy*, *13*, 1–31.

Killian, K. D. (2003). Homogamy outlaws: Interracial couples' strategic responses to racism and partner differences. *Journal of Couple and Relationship Therapy*, *2*, 3–21.

Killian, K. D. (2013). *Interracial couples, intimacy & therapy: Crossing racial borders.* New York, NY: Columbia University Press.

Killian, K. D. (2015). Couple therapy and intercultural relationships. In A. Gurman, J. Lebow, & D. Snyder (Eds.), *Clinical handbook for couple therapy* (5th ed., pp. 512–528). New York, NY: Guilford.

Kim, H., Prouty, A. M., & Roberson, P. N. E. (2012). Narrative therapy with intercultural couples: A case study. *Journal of Family Psychotherapy, 23*(4), 273–286.

Krause, I. B. (1989). The sinking heart: A Punjabi communication of distress. *Social Science and Medicine, 29*, 563–575.

Linehan, M. (1993). *Cognitive-behavioural treatmnent of borderline personality disorder.* New York, NY: Guilford Press.

Llerena-Quinn, R., & Bacigalupe, G. (2009). Constructions of difference among Latino/Latina immigrant and non-Hispanic white couples. In T. A. Karis & K. D. Killian (Eds.), *Intercultural couples. Exploring diversity in intimate relationships* (pp. 167–187). London, UK: Routledge.

Lynch, T. R., Trost, W. T., Salsman, N., & Linehan, M. (2007). Dialectical behavior therapy for borderline personality disorder. *Annual Review of Clinical Psychology, 3*, 181–205.

Malik, R. (2000). Culture and emotions. In C. Squire (Ed.), *Culture in psychology* (pp. 145–160). London, UK: Routledge.

McFadden, J., & Moore, J. L., III (2001). Intercultural marriage and intimacy: Beyond the continental divide. *International Journal for the Advancement of Counselling, 23*, 261–268.

McGoldrick, M., Garcia Preto, N., & Carter, B. (2015). *The expanding family life cycle. Individual, family and social perspectives* (5th ed.). Boston: Allyn & Bacon.

McGoldrick, M., Gerson, R., & Shellenberger, S. (1999). *Genograms: Assessment and intervention.* New York, NY: W. W. Norton.

Molina, B., Estrada, D., & Burnett, J. A. (2004). Cultural communities: Challenges and opportunities in the creation of "happily ever after" stories of intercultural couplehood. *The Family Journal: Counselling and Therapy for Couples and Families, 12*(2), 139–147.

Murphy, C. (2015, June 2). Interfaith marriage is common in the U.S., particularly among the recently wed [Blog post]. Pew Research Centre Survey. Retrieved from https://www.pewresearch.org/fact-tank/2015/06/02/interfaith-marriage/

Nabeshima, E. N. (2005) *Intercultural marriage and early parenting: A qualitative study of American and Japanese couples in the U.S.* Unpublished PhD dissertation: Wright Institute

National Institute of Clinical Excellence. (2009). *Guidelines for depression.* London, UK: Author.

Negy, C., & Snyder, D. K. (2007). Relationship satisfaction of Mexican American and non-Hispanic White American interethnic couples: Issues of acculturation and clinical intervention. *Journal of Marital and Family Therapy, 26*(3), 293–304.

Norton, R. (1983). Measuring marital quality: A critical look at the dependent variable. *Journal of Marriage and the Family, 45*, 141–151.

Okitikpi, T. (2009). *Understanding interracial relationships.* Dorset, UK: Russell House Publishing Ltd.

Osanami Törngren, S., Irastorza, N., & Song, M. (2016). Toward building a conceptual framework on intermarriage. *Ethnicities, 16*(4), 497–520. doi:10.1177/ 1468796816638402

Papadopoulos, R. K. (2002). Refugees, home and trauma. In R. K. Papadopoulos (Ed.), *Therapeutic care for refugees: No place like home* (pp. 9–39). London, UK: Karnac.

Parker, M. L., Johnson, L. N., & Ketring, S. A. (2012). Adult attachment and symptom distress: A dyadic analysis of couple therapy. *Journal of Family Therapy, 34*(3), 321–344.

Pearce, W. B. (2007). *Making social worlds. A communication perspective*. Oxford, UK: Blackwell.

Pearce, W. B., & Cronen, V. E. (1980). *Communication, action and meaning*. Santa Barbara, CA: Praeger.

Perel, E. (2000). A tourist's view of marriage: Cross-cultural couples—Challenges, choices, and implications for therapy. In P. Papp (Ed.), *Couples on the fault line: New directions for therapists* (pp. 187–198). New York, NY: Guilford.

Pilling, S. Roth, A. D., and Stratton, P. (2010) The competences required to deliver effective systemic therapies. Retrieved 3 February, 2009 from Background Documents—Explaining the Framework, Version for Clinicians and Commissioners, from https://www.ucl.ac.uk/pals/research/clinical-educational-and-health-psychology/research-groups/core/competence-frameworks-1

Queer Voices. (2016, February 02). Gay couples more likely to be interracial or inter-ethnic, according to new 2010 census analysis. *Huffpost*. Retrieved June 21, 2018 from https://www.huffingtonpost.com/2012/04/26/gay-couples-interracial-interethnic-2010-census_n_1456613.html.

Reibstein, J., & Burbach, F. (2012). Focusing on coupole therapy: Going forward. *Journal of Family Therapy, 34*(3), 225–228.

Reibstein, J., & Burbach, F. (2013). An increasingly convincing case for couples therapy. *Journal of Family Therapy, 35*(3), 225–228.

Reibstein, J. and Sherbersky, H. (2010) *The manual for practice and research in The Exeter Model*. Unpublished training manual. University of Exeter. CEDAR.

Reibstein, J., & Sherbersky, H. (2012). Behavioural and empathic elements of systemic couple therapy: The Exeter Model and a case study of depression. *Journal of Family Therapy, 34*(3), 271–283.

Reiter, M. J., & Gee, C. B. (2008). Open communication and partner support in intercultural and interfaith romantic relationships: A relational maintenance approach. *Journal of Social and Personal Relationships, 25*(4), 539–559. doi:10.1177/0265407508090872

Roach, A. J., Frazier, C. P., & Bowden, S. R. (1981). The marital satisfaction scale: Development measure intervention research. *Journal of Marriage and Family., 43*(3), 537–546.

Romano, D. (1988). *Intercultural marriage: Promises and pitfalls*. Yarmouth, MA: Intercultural Press Inc.

Romano, D. (2001). *Intercultural marriage: Promises and pitfalls* (2nd ed.). Yarmouth, MA: Intercultural Press Inc.

Rosenblatt, P. C., Karis, T. A., & Powell, R. D. (1995). *Multiracial couples: Black and white voices*. Thousand Oaks, CA: Sage.

Seshadri, G., & Knudson-Martin, C. (2013). How couples manage interracial and intercultural differences: Implications for clinical practice. *Journal of Marital and Family Therapy, 30*(1), 43–58.

Singh, R. (2014). *Love across border control*. Media Diversified.

Singh, R. (2017). *Intimate strangers: Working with interfaith couples. Special issue on spirituality. Australian and New Zealand Journal of Family Therapy, 38*(1), 7–14.

Singh, R., Killian, K. D., Bhugun, D., & Tseng, C. (2020). Clinical work with intercultural couples. In S. Wampler & A. Blow (Eds.), *Systemic family therapy with couples*, The handbook of systemic family therapy (Vol. *3*). Hoboken, NJ: Wiley.

Singla, R. (2015). *Intermarriage and mixed parenting, promoting mental health and well-being: Crossover love*. London, UK: Palgrave Macmillan.

Snyder, D. K. (1979). Multidimensional assessment of marital satisfaction. *Journal of Marriage and the Family, 41*, 813–823. doi:10.2307/351481

Snyder, D. K., & Halford, W. K. (2012). Evidence-basedd couple therapy: Current status and future directions. *Journal of Family Therapy, 34*(3), 229–249.

Spanier, G. B. (1976). Measuring dyadic adjustment: New scales for assessing the quality of marriage and similar dyads. *Journal of Marriage and the Family, 38*(1), 15–28.

Sprenkle, D. H., Davis, S. D., & Lebow, J. L. (2009). *Common factors in couple and family therapy. The overlooked foundation for effective practice*. London, UK: Guilford Press.

Stratton, P., Reibstein, J., Lask, J., Singh, R., & Asen, E. (2011). Competences and occupational standards for systemic family and couple therapy. *Journal of Family Therapy, 33*(2), 123–143.

Sullivan, C., & Cottone, R. R. (2006). Culture based couple therapy and intercultural relationships: A review of the literature. *The Family Journal, 14*(3), 221–225.

Tamura, T., & Lau, A. (1992). Connectedness versus separateness: Applicability of family therapy to Japanese families. *Family Process, 31*(4), 319–340.

Ting-Toomey, S. (1999). *Communicating across cultures*. New York, NY: Guilford.

Tomm, K. (1998). *A question of perspective. Journal of Marital and Family Therapy, 24*(4), 409–413.

Tseng, S. T. (2016). *How do intercultural couples perceive and deal with cultural differences in their relationship over time—A snapshot of three couples in Taiwan* (MSc dissertation). University of Bedfordshire, UK.

United Nations Population Fund Report. (2000). *The state of the world population. Lives together, worlds apart. Men and women in a time of change*. New York, NY: United Nations.

Waldman, K., & Rubalcava, L. (2005). Psychotherapy with intercultural couples: A contemporary psychodynamic approach. *The American Journal of Psychotherapy, 59*(3), 227–245.

Wallis, J., & Singh, R. (2014). Constructions and enactments of whiteness: A discursive analysis. *Journal of Family Therapy, 36*(S1), 39–64.

Author Index

The Intercultural Exeter Couples Model: Making Connections for a Divided World Through Systemic-Behavioral Therapy, First Edition. Janet Reibstein and Reenee Singh.
© 2021 John Wiley & Sons Ltd. Published 2021 by John Wiley & Sons Ltd.

Subject Index

The Intercultural Exeter Couples Model: Making Connections for a Divided World Through Systemic-Behavioral Therapy, First Edition. Janet Reibstein and Reenee Singh.
© 2021 John Wiley & Sons Ltd. Published 2021 by John Wiley & Sons Ltd.